Cambridge Elements

Elements in Ethics
edited by
Ben Eggleston
University of Kansas
Dale E. Miller
Old Dominion University, Virginia

SUBJECTIVE VERSUS OBJECTIVE MORAL WRONGNESS

Peter A. Graham
University of Massachusetts Amherst

CAMBRIDGE
UNIVERSITY PRESS

CAMBRIDGE
UNIVERSITY PRESS

University Printing House, Cambridge CB2 8BS, United Kingdom

One Liberty Plaza, 20th Floor, New York, NY 10006, USA

477 Williamstown Road, Port Melbourne, VIC 3207, Australia

314–321, 3rd Floor, Plot 3, Splendor Forum, Jasola District Centre,
New Delhi – 110025, India

79 Anson Road, #06–04/06, Singapore 079906

Cambridge University Press is part of the University of Cambridge.

It furthers the University's mission by disseminating knowledge in the pursuit of
education, learning, and research at the highest international levels of excellence.

www.cambridge.org
Information on this title: www.cambridge.org/9781108706612
DOI: 10.1017/9781108588249

First published 2021

A catalogue record for this publication is available from the British Library.

ISBN 978-1-108-70661-2 Paperback
ISSN 2516-4031 (online)
ISSN 2516-4023 (print)

Subjective versus Objective Moral Wrongness

Elements in Ethics

DOI: 10.1017/9781108588249
First published online: March 2021

Peter A. Graham
University of Massachusetts Amherst
Author for correspondence: Peter A. Graham, pgraham@umass.edu

Abstract: Presently, there is a debate between Subjectivists and Objectivists about moral wrongness. Subjectivism is the view that the moral status of our actions, whether they are morally wrong or not, is grounded in our subjective circumstances – either our beliefs about, or our evidence concerning, the world around us. Objectivism, on the other hand, is the view that the moral status of our actions is grounded in our objective circumstances – all those facts other than those that comprise our subjective circumstances. A third view, Ecumenism, has it that the moral status of our actions is grounded both in our subjective and our objective circumstances. After outlining and evaluating the various arguments against both Subjectivism and Objectivism, the Element offers a tentative defense of Objectivism about moral wrongness.

Keywords: moral permissibility, perspectivism, subjective moral wrongness, objective moral wrongness, "ought"

ISBNs: 9781108706612 (PB), 9781108588249 (OC)
ISSNs: 2516-4031 (online), 2516-4023 (print)

Contents

1 Subjectivism, Objectivism, and Ecumenism

The debate between Subjectivists and Objectivists about moral wrongness is a debate about what kinds of facts the moral status of an agent's action – whether it is morally wrong or not – is true in virtue of, or is grounded in.[1] The terms "Subjectivism" and "Objectivism," however, need precisifying.

As the Subjectivism/Objectivism debate is a debate about what facts the moral status of an action is grounded in, the first question to ask is: What are the different sets of facts participants to the debate are in dispute about? Subjectivists think that the relevant facts are those that constitute the agent's subjective circumstances, whereas Objectivists think the relevant facts are those that constitute the agent's objective circumstances. Roughly speaking, one's subjective circumstances just are all the facts concerning how the world seems to be from one's perspective. And, roughly speaking, one's objective circumstances just are all the facts concerning how the world actually is, independent of how things seem to be from one's perspective. As I'm understanding it, then, the set of facts that constitute a person's objective circumstances is the complement of that which constitutes their subjective circumstances – if a certain fact is among an agent's subjective circumstances, then it is not among their objective circumstances, and if a certain fact is not among an agent's subjective circumstances, then it is among their objective circumstances.[2]

Subjectivisms can vary depending on the way in which "how the world seems to be from the agent's perspective" is interpreted. *Belief Subjectivists* maintain that an agent's subjective circumstances comprise all the facts there are about what they believe about the world around them. *Evidence Subjectivists* contend that an agent's subjective circumstances comprise all the facts there are about what their evidence about the world around them is. For much of what follows, the distinction between Belief Subjectivism and Evidence Subjectivism won't much matter, but it is important to keep in mind that different Subjectivists take

---

[1] The notion of grounding is supposed to capture this "in virtue of" thought. A grounding relation is thus supposed to be a one-way asymmetric necessary determination relation stronger than, though entailing, supervenience. Modern classics on the nature and logic of this grounding relation are Rosen (2010) and Fine (2012).

[2] What about facts that are conjunctions and disjunctions of facts both in an agent's subjective circumstances and their objective circumstances? For example, take either the conjunction [(*S* believes that snow is white) & (snow is white)] or the disjunction [(*S*'s evidence indicates that snow is white) ∨ (snow is white)]. How should we classify these propositions? Though this is an interesting question, it isn't one that makes any important difference for the arguments I shall be considering. For this reason, we could, by stipulation, treat both conjunctions and disjunctions of combinations of subjective and objective facts as subjective facts. (The issue here is clearly related to those that surround A. N. Prior's [1960] famous demonstration that an "ought"-claim can indeed be derived from an "is"-claim.)

different stances on the kinds of subjective circumstances they take to be the ground of moral wrongness.[3]

The easiest way to get a grip on what is in dispute between Objectivists and Subjectivists about moral wrongness is to consider a case about which they disagree:

> <u>Switch</u>: Gomez is looking for her wallet. Chen stands near the light switch and can flip it, thereby turning on the light and helping Gomez in her search for her wallet. Chen believes, and all of her evidence indicates, that were she to flip the light switch, all that would happen is that the light would go on and Gomez would be helped in her search for her wallet. In actual fact, the light switch has been hooked up to a bomb which will go off, killing twenty innocent people, if Chen flips it.

Subjectivists generally maintain that it would not be morally wrong for Chen to flip the switch in *Switch* – from Chen's perspective, flipping the switch will hurt no one and help Gomez find her wallet. Objectivists, on the other hand, generally maintain that it would be morally wrong for Chen to flip the switch in *Switch* – flipping the switch will cause twenty innocent people to be killed and it is morally wrong to kill innocent people when one can avoid doing so.

Having gotten a flavor of what's in dispute in the Subjectivism/Objectivism debate, I'll now more carefully consider each of the possible positions in this debate one might take. Subjectivists maintain that the moral status of an agent's action is grounded in their subjective circumstances. But because a fact can be either fully or partially grounded in some other set of facts, we need first to distinguish between two theses that might legitimately claim the mantle "Subjectivism":

Subjectivism: the moral status of an agent's action is *fully grounded* in their subjective circumstances.

Ecumenism: the moral status of an agent's action is *merely partially grounded* in their subjective circumstances.

---

[3] There is an in-depth discussion of the various different kinds of Subjectivism in Driver (2012). Some of those I call "Subjectivists" others sometimes call "Perspectivists" (Kiesewetter 2011, 2017; Lord 2015). Others sometimes use "Subjectivism" to pick out what I do by "Belief Subjectivism" (Zimmerman 2008, 2014). There is some reason to use "Perspectivism" to pick out what I pick out by "Subjectivism" just because there are a number of different views in ethics, and philosophy more generally, that might well be called "Subjectivist." (According to some views, a moral theory counts as "Subjectivist" just in case according to it the moral status of an action is partially grounded in motivational features of the agent at the time of its performance. That is not the sense of "Subjectivism" I am employing.) However, I stick with the "Subjectivism/ Objectivism" terminology because I think it connects up more broadly with views that have been called versions of "Subjectivism" throughout the literature on this particular debate about moral wrongness.

To say that the moral status of an agent's action is fully grounded in their subjective circumstances is to say that every one of the facts that altogether ground the moral status of the agent's action are facts in their subjective circumstances. To say that the moral status of an agent's action is merely partially grounded in their subjective circumstances is to say that some of the facts that altogether ground the moral status of the agent's action are facts in their subjective circumstances, while some of the facts that altogether ground the status of the agent's action are facts that are not in their subjective circumstances. (Clearly, given how we've defined an agent's subjective and objective circumstances, Ecumenists hold that the moral status of an agent's action is merely partially grounded in their objective circumstances as well.) Though some might claim that endorsing anything as strong as Ecumenism is enough to count one as a Subjectivist, for the purposes of our discussion only those who endorse Subjectivism, along the lines defined above, according to which even merely partial grounding in an agent's objective circumstances is ruled out, will count as Subjectivists.

The definition of Objectivism follows naturally:

Objectivism: the moral status of an agent's action is *fully grounded* in their objective circumstances.

Just as our initial definition of "Subjectivism" has it that the moral status of an agent's actions is fully grounded in their subjective circumstances, this definition of "Objectivism," correspondingly, has it that the moral status of an agent's actions is fully grounded in their objective circumstances.

So understood, Ecumenism and Objectivism are both incompatible with Subjectivism and with each other. Our three positions are mutually exclusive and mutually exhaustive. Anything other than full grounding of the moral status of an agent's action in their subjective circumstances is incompatible with Subjectivism. No grounding, either full or merely partial, of the moral status of an agent's action in anything other than their objective circumstances is compatible with Objectivism. And only merely partial grounding of the moral status of an agent's action in their subjective circumstances is necessary and sufficient for the truth of Ecumenism. In what follows, I shall offer a qualified defense of Objectivism. In particular, I'll consider various arguments first against Subjectivism and then against Objectivism. Though there are arguments that do seem to establish the falsity of Subjectivism, none of the arguments against Objectivism definitively show it to be false. Now, for all that will be said, it might well be that one of the arguments against Objectivism does in fact go through, in which case it would be some form of Ecumenism that is true. As it is unclear whether any of those arguments do succeed, all that will be offered is merely a qualified defense of Objectivism.

The debate between Subjectivists, Objectivists, and Ecumenists is of fundamental significance.[4] Whether what I may permissibly do is grounded in how things seem to me or in how the world actually is, or in both, is of paramount importance for moral theory. If Subjectivism is true, then a whole swath of moral theories, including, for instance, all forms of Objective Consequentialism – the view according to which any option one has that fails to maximize value, of all the options one has, is morally wrong – are ruled out simply as a matter of course. It should be a top priority, then, to settle this question before embarking on an in-depth investigation into the grounds of moral wrongness, so that we don't go wrong in the very first step of our investigation.[5]

2 The Sense-Splitting Reply

Some don't see the Subjectivism/Objectivism debate as being of deep moral significance. They are inclined to think that trying to settle this dispute is a fool's errand because the debate between Subjectivists and Objectivists about moral wrongness is in fact much ado about nothing. They diagnose the debate as grounded in a confusion. The confusion is about wrongness itself – in particular, the confusion involves thinking that there is a single notion of wrongness about which Subjectivists and Objectivists are disagreeing. Rather, so goes this reply, Subjectivists and Objectivists are just talking past each other because they are each concerned with a distinct kind of wrongness. There is a subjective notion of wrongness and an objective notion of wrongness, and each side of the debate is correct about their respective notions of wrongness.[6]

This sense-splitting reply misses its mark. Whether there are subjective and objective notions of wrongness or not, we can pin down the notion of wrongness about which Subjectivists and Objectivists are in dispute, and it is clear, once it is

---

[4] Examples of Subjectivists, in the sense I've argued for here, are Prichard (2002), Ross (1939), and Howard-Snyder (2005). Objectivists include Moore (1912), Ross (2002), Feldman (1986), Thomson (1990), and Graham (2010). Jackson (1991) is an Ecumenist because he thinks that moral wrongness is grounded both in the agent's beliefs about nonmoral matters and in the objective values of the states of affairs the agent believes to obtain. Zimmerman (2008, 2014) and Kiesewetter (2011, 2017) are predominantly subjective Ecumenists because, though they think that the moral wrongness of an action is primarily a function of the agent's evidence, they think it is also a function of the options the agent has available to them, and what those options are is an objective fact. Zimmerman (2008, 2014) uses the term "Prospectivism" to pick out the kind of predominantly subjective Ecumenism he favors. Another proponent of Prospectivism is Mason (2013).

[5] Similar issues to those that divide Subjectivists, Objectivists, and Ecumenists also arise within the literature on normative reasons and normative "oughts" (both practical and epistemic), including Sepielli (2012, 2018), Kiesewetter (2011), Lockhart (2000), Lord (2017, 2018), and Way and Whiting (2016, 2017).

[6] This sense-splitting strategy is employed to in Sepielli (2012).

so pinned down, that they are not talking past each other. What, then, is the notion of wrongness about which Subjectivists and Objectivists are in dispute? It is that of which we are trying to give an account when doing moral theory (i.e., it is the notion of wrongness about which Kantians and Utilitarians disagree when they give their respective accounts of moral wrongness). And that notion of wrongness is the notion of wrongness that is of ultimate concern to the morally conscientious person when in their deliberations about what to do they ask themself, "What would be morally wrong for me to do in this situation?".[7] The morally conscientious person, who asks themself this question in their deliberations about what to do, isn't actually asking themself two distinct questions. Nor are they muddle-headedly thinking in terms of some confused amalgam of two distinct questions. No. There is one unambiguous question they are asking themself. And, thus, there is only one notion of wrongness they are ultimately concerned about when in their deliberations about what to do they want to avoid doing something morally wrong. It is *that* notion of wrongness about which Subjectivists and Objectivists are in dispute. In other, more explicit words, Subjectivists think that the notion of wrongness that is of ultimate concern to the morally conscientious person when, in their deliberations about what to do, they ask themself, "What would be morally wrong for me to do?", is one that is grounded solely in facts in their subjective circumstances. Objectivists, on the other hand, think that the notion of wrongness that the morally conscientious agent is asking about when they ask themself that question is one that is not grounded in any facts in their subjective circumstances. And Ecumenists think that the kind of wrongness with which the morally conscientious agent is ultimately concerned in their deliberations about what to do is grounded in a combination of their subjective and objective circumstances. As we can independently anchor the one and only notion of wrongness about which Subjectivists, Objectivists, and Ecumenists are in dispute to the notion of wrongness about which the morally conscientious agent is ultimately concerned in their deliberations about what to do, the sense-splitting reply to the Subjectivism/ Objectivism debate collapses. There *is* a unique notion of wrongness about which the parties are disagreeing and theirs is very much a live dispute.[8]

---

[7] It is important to distinguish the morally conscientious person from the morally virtuous person, or the moral person *simpliciter*. A morally conscientious person is one who is particularly concerned, punctiliously so, about moral wrongness. They are concerned to avoid wrongdoing. They needn't be concerned about anything like maximizing value (unless they happen to be a Consequentialist). Nor need they be at all interested in going above and beyond the call of moral duty; doing the morally supererogatory isn't something one need be concerned about to count as morally conscientious. Zimmerman (2008) is the first to note that it is the deliberations of the morally conscientious agent in particular that are central to the Subjectivism/Objectivism debate.

[8] This response to the sense-splitting reply is employed in Zimmerman (2008). A version of this reply is also to be found in Kiesewetter (2011, 2017) and Lord (2015, 2018).

3 Against Objectivism

There are a number of different arguments against strict Objectivism about moral wrongness. In this section, I survey and evaluate the prospects of various of these arguments. My conclusion is that none of these arguments against Objectivism is conclusive.

3.1 The Brute Intuition Argument against Objectivism

One of the most popular arguments against Objectivism involves a brute appeal to intuition: it is not morally wrong for Chen to flip the light switch in *Switch*, but, as it would be morally wrong for Chen to flip it in that case if Objectivism were true, Objectivism is false. This argument is simple and straightforward. It is also, however, not very dialectically effective. Objectivists simply reject the intuition that Chen does not act morally wrongly in flipping the switch in *Switch*. True, Chen acts blamelessly in doing so, but that's just an instance of blameless wrongdoing. And according to Objectivists, blameless wrongdoing is ubiquitous. For instance, for the Objectivist, when I walk off with your jacket, one that is identical to my own, by mistake from the cloakroom, I wrongly violate your right against me that I not interfere with your property. But because there was no way I could have known that I was taking your jacket (suppose that that is the case in this scenario), I'm not to blame for taking it. In such a case, indignation toward me on the part of others on account of my behaving the way I did would be totally out of place.[9] Chen's flipping the switch in *Switch* is, for the Objectivist, just another instance, though one with more disastrous consequences, of this more general kind of blameless wrongdoing.[10]

Not only can there be blameless wrongdoing, the Objectivist will say, there can even be cases in which one would be blameworthy for failing to do that which it is morally wrong for one to do. Chen, for instance, not only would not be blameworthy for flipping the switch in *Switch*, but she would, in fact, be blameworthy for not flipping it. Given that she believes, and all of her evidence indicates, that flipping the switch will do nothing but help Gomez, and, in

---

[9] In arguing on the Objectivist's behalf here, I'm implicitly appealing to something like a Strawsonian conception of moral blameworthiness (Strawson 1962), one according to which a person is blameworthy for doing something if and only if it would be appropriate for one of the blame emotions – guilt, resentment, and indignation – to be borne toward them on account of their doing that thing. For recent developments of this approach to moral blameworthiness see Wallace (1994), Graham (2014), and Rosen (2015). Though I appeal to this conception of moral blameworthiness here, a similar point could be made, I think, with respect to other non-emotion-centered conceptions of moral blameworthiness, like those of Zimmerman (1988) and Scanlon (2008).

[10] The Objectivist maneuver of distinguishing wrongdoing and blameworthiness is most famously deployed by Moore (1912).

general, she morally ought to help Gomez if she can do so at no cost to her or anyone else, it would be morally blameworthy for Chen to refrain from flipping the switch, even though doing so would, according to the Objectivist, be morally wrong. For the Objectivist, then, moral wrongness and moral blame-worthiness can, and often do, come apart drastically. Because of this, the argument against Objectivism consisting in the brute appeal to the intuition that it would not be morally wrong for Chen to flip the switch in *Switch* is particularly dialectically ineffective.

3.2 The Action-Guiding/Usability Argument against Objectivism

Another argument against Objectivism appeals to the thought that to be true a moral theory must be action-guiding.[11] The thought is that being inherently practical, as opposed to merely theoretical, morality, of necessity, must provide agents with guidance about what to do in any situation in which they might find themselves. Because the truth of Objectivism about moral wrongness would render morality incapable of carrying out this function, so goes this argument, Objectivism is false. (It is important to this argument that morality must neces-sarily be *universally* action-guiding, in that it must provide guidance in all cases, including ones in which agents don't have full knowledge of their situation. This is because in cases of full knowledge, presumably, objective moral theories are no less action-guiding than are subjective ones.) The correct moral theory must be *usable* in helping one determine what to do. Knowing the principles that deter-mine moral rightness and wrongness cannot leave one hopelessly helpless in the face of ignorance and uncertainty. But that's precisely the position one would often find oneself in were Objectivism true. So, Objectivism is false.

This argument may be persuasive from a distance. But upon closer inspection its weaknesses are manifest. First, though it is affirmed both that to be true a moral theory must be action-guiding and that Objectivist moral theories are clearly not action-guiding, usually very little is said either about what it means for a moral theory to be action-guiding or about why it is that Objectivist moral theories can't be action-guiding in that sense.[12] What exactly does it mean to say that a moral theory must be usable for it to be true? Usable how? And by whom? Unless these questions can be satisfactorily answered, this argument against Objectivism is at best a promissory note, and at worst a mirage.

---

[11] A recent attempt at this style of argument is Fox (2019).

[12] A notable exception is Smith (2018). Smith goes into very particular detail about what it means to say that a moral theory is usable and why it is that purely objective moral theories fail to be usable in the relevant sense. Though Smith is clear about what it takes for a moral theory to be usable, it is less clear whether she establishes that morality must indeed be usable in that sense for it to be true.

Take, for example, the question: by whom must a moral theory be usable for it to be usable in the sense necessary for its being true? Consider a very small child who doesn't possess the concepts of moral rightness and wrongness. It is dubious whether, for any sense of "usable," *any* moral theory could be usable by such a child. Presumably, then, a moral theory needn't be usable by anyone for it to be true. So, maybe to be true a moral theory need only be usable by those who possess the concepts employed in the principles that constitute it.[13] Arguably, morality only applies to those who possess the concepts of rightness and wrongness; that is, the only beings who can act morally rightly or wrongly are ones who possess those concepts, and so, perhaps, because of that, those for whom a moral theory must be usable for it to be true are all and only those who possess the concepts of rightness and wrongness.[14] But consider another person – someone who, though they possess all the relevant concepts, invariably makes logical mistakes whenever they derive particular consequences from general principles. Arguably, for such a person no moral theory would be usable, for any sense of "usable." Okay. So maybe the usability requirement is meant to exclude such agents; perhaps a moral theory must be usable by a minimally idealized rational agent who possesses the concepts employed in it. That may be a defensible restriction, but what exactly is the relevant idealization and is it consistent with the motivation, whatever it happens to be, for the thought that moral theories must be usable, or action-guiding, for them to be true? This is not so easy a question to answer, for the motivation for the usability criterion is often unspecified.

Consider also the question *how* a theory must be usable for it to be true. What does it mean for a moral theory's principles to be usable by an agent? What counts as a person's using a moral theory to determine what to do? Must it be the case that for any situation in which one might find oneself one is able to determine or deduce from the theory what to do in that situation? Presumably not, for in many cases there will be no action that the moral theory dictates that the agent must perform. Take, for instance, my choice of having either orange juice or apple juice with my breakfast this morning. Many moral theories surely are no help to me in deciding this question. Does that make them not usable? That would be implausible. Maybe it need only be the case that a theory be such that one can use it to decide what to do in cases in which the theory requires that one do some particular thing. The choice between orange and apple juice, being

---

[13] This presumably requires more than just the possession of the concepts of rightness and wrongness, for a person who possessed those concepts but who lacked the non-deontic concepts in which the theory declared them to be grounded could just as well not use that theory as if they lacked the concepts of rightness and wrongness themselves.

[14] That morality only applies to those who possess the concepts of rightness and wrongness is often thought to explain the widely held belief that it is conceptually impossible for very small children and most nonhuman animals to act rightly or wrongly.

one that no plausible moral theory would take a stand on, isn't a choice situation in which a moral theory needs to be usable in determining what to do for it to count as usable in the relevant sense. But a choice between doing that which would maximize utility and that which would keep a promise very plausibly is one that a plausible moral theory will take a stand on; that is, it is one for which the moral theory will dictate that one is required to do one or required to do the other. But consider a theory according to which, because the relevant moral factors balance out, both keeping the promise and maximizing utility were deemed permissible. Would such a moral theory be unusable in this situation? That is, would it be the case that because one couldn't figure out what to do in the situation from the moral theory that the theory is not universally usable? Again, that would be implausible.

Crucially, for the proponent of the usability argument against Objectivism, moral theories, to be true, must be usable in situations of uncertainty. But it's not so clear that a purely objective moral theory can't be usable in situations of uncertainty. Suppose Lopez faces a choice between pressing a certain button and doing nothing and she knows that pressing the button will have a 50 percent chance of producing more utility than her doing nothing and a 50 percent chance of doing nothing. In such a case, it seems Lopez most certainly *can* use Objective Utilitarianism – according to which what she morally ought to do is maximize utility – to determine what to do in this situation; viz., press the button. In fact, if Lopez is uncertain what to do because she is uncertain which moral theory is true, then comes to believe Objective Utilitarianism, and, then, because of that belief, is moved to press the button, then surely she has used Objective Utilitarianism in deciding what to do. But if she's used the theory to decide what to do in her situation, then the theory is usable for her in deciding what to do in that situation involving uncertainty.

But even if an objective moral theory can be usable in some situations of uncertainty, does it follow that an objective moral theory can be usable in *all possible* situations of uncertainty? Well, again, it all depends on how one understands what it is to use a moral theory to determine what to do. On one understanding of that notion, arguably, objective moral theories are indeed usable. Begin with an analogy. Take the purely self-interested person – one who is solely concerned with their own well-being – facing a choice under conditions of uncertainty about the outcomes of their various options. Suppose this person doesn't have a settled view as to what the correct theory of well-being – a theory of that in virtue of which a person is as well off as they are – is. Then suppose they come to accept hedonism – the theory according to which how well off one is is a straightforward function of the pleasures and pains in one's life – as the correct theory of well-being. They then rationally use the various evaluations of their well-being in the various possible outcomes of each of their options as inputs into some reasonable decision theory, and choose that option which is the output of that decision theory. In this case, it surely seems as if the purely self-interested person has in fact used hedonism to help them determine what to do in their situation of uncertainty. But, and here's the point, hedonism is a purely objective theory of well-being – it doesn't tie an agent's well-being either to their beliefs about, or their evidence concerning, the world around them. So, purely objective theories of well-being can be used in situations of uncertainty to help purely self-interested persons decide what to do, and thus purely objective theories of well-being can be usable in such situations. Now, why should the case of the morally conscientious person and objective moral theories be any different? If a morally conscientious person takes whatever objective moral theory they believe to be true and inputs its verdicts about the various possible outcomes of their different options into a reasonable decision theory, and then chooses that option which is the output of that theory, then how have they not used that purely objective moral theory to help them determine what to do?

The proponent of the usability argument against Objectivism is likely to protest here that in the situation as described, the morally conscientious person has not *solely* used the purely objective moral theory to determine what to do, but rather has instead used the theory *and the reasonable decision theory* together to determine what to do. Maybe, they might maintain, for a moral theory to be usable in a situation it must be the case that an agent can use the theory, *and the theory alone*, to determine what to do in their situation. But this can't really be the criterion, for even subjective moral theories are not such that one can use them *alone* to determine what to do in one's situation. Even subjective moral theories have to be coupled with deductive reasoning – modus ponens, modus tollens, etc. – for anyone to use them to determine what to do. But if, to be usable in the sense necessary to be true, according to the usability argument against Objectivism, a moral theory can be used in conjunction with deductive reasoning to determine for an agent what to do in any situation in which they find themself, then why too couldn't a moral theory count as usable in the sense required for it to be true if it can, in conjunction with reasoning in accord with a reasonable decision theory, determine for an agent what to do in any situation in which they find themself? In other words, if deductive reasoning is allowed in, then why can't reasoning in accord with a reasonable decision theory be let in too? The proponent of the usability objection to Objectivism hasn't yet motivated an account of usability that is both plausible and which rules out objective moral theories as unusable in situations of uncertainty.[15]

---

[15] One common response to the Action-Guiding/Usability argument against Objectivism is to endorse a "two-level" moral theory. This approach is favored by Feldman (2012) and Smith (2018). As Feldman puts it, a two-level moral theory is one that incorporates into it both a "theoretical-level

3.3 Lord's Argument against Objectivism

Lord (2015) offers an argument against Objectivism that is related to, but importantly different from, the action-guidance argument just considered. According to Lord's Argument, for one to be morally obligated to do something it must be the case that one has the ability to do that thing *for the right reasons*. But, so argues Lord, one can only be able to do something for the right reasons if those reasons are in one's epistemic ken. And so, for one to be morally obligated to do something, the reasons in virtue of which one is so obligated must be in one's epistemic ken. As Objectivism has it that one can be morally obligated to do something without the reasons for why one is so obligated being in one's epistemic ken (e.g., Objectivism has it that Chen is morally obliged not to flip the switch in *Switch* even though the reasons why she is morally obliged not to flip the switch – viz., that doing so will kill twenty innocent people – are not in her epistemic ken), concludes Lord, Objectivism is false. This argument is similar to but different from the action-guidance argument previously considered, for though it does purport to connect what one is morally obligated to do with what's in one's epistemic ken by way of a requirement that one be *able to be guided* by the reasons that obligate one to act in the way one is obligated to act, it doesn't appeal to some independent thought about the necessary usability of a moral theory.

Lord's Argument can be stated more rigorously as follows:

(1) If A is obligated to ϕ, then A has the ability to ϕ for the right reasons.
(2) If A has the ability to ϕ for the right reasons, then A epistemically possesses the right reasons for A's ϕing.
(3) Therefore, if A is obligated to ϕ, then A epistemically possesses the right reasons for A's ϕing.

The first premise of this argument Lord calls the Right Reasons Ability Condition (RRAC).

In support of the RRAC Lord offers two considerations. First, he claims that there is an important connection between creditworthiness and acting for the reasons that make so acting permissible. That is, he claims that the following is true:

---

principle" and a "practical-level principle," the former giving a "criterion of rightness/wrongness" and the latter providing a usable "decision guide" for agents to use in situations of uncertainty. It is hard to know exactly how to characterize proponents of two-level moral theories. Are they Objectivists, Subjectivists, Ecumenists, or proponents of the sense-splitting reply to the Subjectivism/Objectivism debate? Part of the reason it is hard to describe what views such proponents of two-level theories endorse is that the questions they take themselves to be seeking answers to seem to be different from that to which Subjectivists, Objectivists, and Ecumenists are seeking an answer; viz., what is the sense of "wrong" in the concern of the morally conscientious person, in their deliberations about what to do, not to act wrongly.

Credit: A's φing is creditworthy if and only if A φs for the reasons that make φing permissible.

If Credit is true and RRAC is false, it will follow that there can be cases in which one is morally obligated to φ even though it is impossible for one's token φing to be creditworthy. And that, so claims Lord, is implausible. Second, Lord maintains that if RRAC is false, then there will be possible cases in which one is obligated to φ but can't nonaccidentally φ for the very reasons that make it the case that one is so obligated. In such cases one would thus have to get lucky to do what one is obligated to do. Because it must always be possible for one to nonaccidentally, and thus nonluckily, do that which one is obligated to do for the reasons that obligate one to do it, RRAC must be true.

Though Lord also offers reasons in support of the second premise of his argument, the one other than RRAC, I think it is enough to see that Lord's motivations for RRAC don't support it to show that his argument against Objectivism fails. Consider the motivations for RRAC that Lord offers in turn. First, does *Credit* support RRAC? I think not. First, it seems that one can be morally creditworthy for doing something when, in fact, there are *no* reasons that make that action permissible. Suppose Chang is drowning and Nguyen can save him by pressing a certain button. Suppose also that pressing the button will cause Nguyen to lose her right leg. Suppose also that the loss of Nguyen's right leg is not a cost that she is morally obligated to bear to save Chang from drowning; pressing the button and saving Chang is supererogatory – that is, it would be morally permissible for Nguyen not to press the button. Suppose, finally, that she does press the button. Her saving Chang from drowning at the cost to her of her leg is, it seems, a creditworthy action on Nguyen's part. However, plausibly, there aren't any reasons that *make* Nguyen's saving of Chang permissible. True, there are reasons for which Nguyen saved Chang – let's suppose that the fact it would save Chang's life, which is valuable, is the reason for which Nguyen presses the button and saves Chang – but those reasons aren't what make Nguyen's pressing the button permissible. *Nothing makes* Nguyen's pressing the button morally permissible. Plausibly, for some reasons to make an action permissible it must be the case that absent those reasons that action wouldn't be permissible. But that's false in this case: were it not the case that Nguyen's pressing the button would save Chang's life, it need not be the case that Nguyen's pressing the button would be morally impermissible. Suppose that were it not the case that pressing the button would save Chang's life that would be because Chang wasn't drowning, say. In such a case, Nguyen's pressing the button, and thereby sacrificing her leg, would not be impermissible. True, her doing so would be highly imprudent, but it wouldn't be morally impermissible. So, we have a counterexample to **Credit**: Nguyen's pressing of the button is creditworthy, but she doesn't do so for the reasons that make her doing so morally permissible, because there are no reasons that make her pressing the button permissible.

For another counterexample of this sort, suppose Khan gives Hussein her one and only lollipop because Hussein has asked her for it. Let's suppose that Khan is not morally required to give Hussein the lollipop. Here, again, it seems we have a creditworthy act, but nothing *makes* it permissible. The fact that Hussein asked her for a lollipop is the reason for which Khan gives it to her, but that reason doesn't *make* her giving him the lollipop permissible, for her giving him the lollipop wouldn't have been impermissible were that not to have been the case.[16]

Second, there seem to be counterexamples to **Credit** even when it seems that there are reasons that make the relevant morally permissible act permissible. Take once again the case in which Chang is drowning and Nguyen can save him by pressing a certain button, the pressing of which will also cause Nguyen to lose her right leg. In this case it is intuitive that it is permissible both for Nguyen to press the button and for her to refrain from pressing the button. And, intuitively, what makes refraining from pressing the button permissible is the fact that pressing it will cause Nguyen to lose her leg. Now suppose Nguyen refrains from pressing the button because pressing it will cost her her leg. She retains her leg and Chang drowns. Intuitively, Nguyen's refraining from pressing the button is not a particularly creditworthy act (in fact, it's neither blameworthy nor praiseworthy), but she performs it for the reasons that make her act morally permissible. So, that would seem to be a counterexample to **Credit**.

Finally, there is a third type of case that is a counterexample to **Credit**. Consider:

> *Disjunction*: After investigating her situation, Nguyen knows that she has either promised Mbeki to ϕ at t_1 or that ϕing at t_1 will maximize happiness, but not both. Nguyen also knows that ϕing at t_1 will cost her a significant amount – the loss of her leg, say. Nguyen also knows that if either she did promise Mbeki to ϕ at t_1 or her ϕing at t_1 will maximize happiness, then she morally ought to ϕ at t_1. Last, in fact, Nguyen has not promised Mbeki to ϕ at t_1 but her ϕing at t_1 will maximize happiness.

---

[16] Even if this counterfactual test for whether a consideration makes an action permissible is doubted, it nonetheless remains intuitive in this case (and the case involving Nguyen and Chang) that nothing makes the relevant action morally permissible. It's not the kind of action that needs any consideration at all to make it morally permissible. Furthermore, it is intuitive that the fact Hussein asked for Khan's lollipop isn't any part of what makes Khan's giving it to her morally permissible. If anything, Khan's giving her the lollipop is morally permissible not for any reason whatsoever, but rather by default.

It seems that in this case Nguyen might ϕ at t_1 and her doing so might well be creditworthy. However, in *Disjunction* Nguyen does not ϕ for the reasons that make ϕing permissible. If any, the reasons that make her ϕing permissible in this case are that her ϕing will maximize happiness. But that's not the reason for which she ϕs. Rather, she ϕs for the reason that either she promised Mbeki to ϕ at t_1 or her ϕing at t_1 will maximize happiness, and that disjunctive fact is not the reason that makes her ϕing permissible. (To count the disjunctive fact as being a reason that makes ϕing permissible would, at best, be an objectionable form of over-counting.) So, once again, ***Credit*** is false.

That's the ***Credit***-based motivation for RRAC that Lord offers. What about the second motivation he offers for it? Must it really be the case that for one to be morally obligated to do something, one must be able to nonaccidentally do that thing for the very reasons that one is so obligated to do it? It seems not. There seem to be numerous cases where it is plausible that one might be morally obligated to ϕ even though in one's particular situation one is unable to nonaccidentally ϕ for the reasons that make one obligated to ϕ. Take the case of moral testimony. Suppose pressing a certain button will save an innocent person from drowning but I have no evidence that this is the case. If a very reliable third party told me that what I'm morally obligated to do is press the button but refrained from explaining why that's so, it's intuitive that I would be morally obligated to press the button, but I couldn't nonaccidentally press the button for the reason that makes me obligated to – viz., that doing so will save someone from drowning. Were I to press the button for that reason, it would be just a matter of luck that I pressed the button for the very reason that made it the case that I was obligated to do so. Or take *Disjunction* once again. In that case it seems that Nguyen is morally obligated to ϕ even though she can't, given her epistemic situation, nonaccidentally ϕ for the very reason, r, which makes it true that she is morally obligated to ϕ – viz., that her ϕing will maximize happiness. She can't nonaccidentally ϕ in this case because were she to ϕ for the reason that ϕing will maximize happiness, her ϕing for the right reasons would just be a matter of luck.

Now Lord might contend that the reason why I'm morally obligated to press the button in the testimony case is not that pressing the button would save a person from drowning, but rather that the reliable third party told me I was obligated to. And he might also suggest that the reason why Nguyen is morally obligated to ϕ in *Disjunction* is not r, that doing so would maximize happiness, but rather the disjunction, that ϕ-ing will either keep a promise or maximize happiness. If these were the reasons that obligate in the two cases, then, arguably, my pressing the button in the testimony case and Nguyen's ϕ-ing in *Disjunction* needn't be cases in which we can only accidentally do what we're morally obligated to do for the reasons that obligate us in these cases. But treating the reasons why we are obligated in these cases in these ways is already to presuppose a non-Objectivist account of the reasons that morally obligate people to do what they are morally obligated to do. For these purported obligating reasons are purportedly obligating only in virtue of their relations to the subjective states of the agents in question — the third party's testimony only counts as an obligating reason, if it does, in virtue of its giving me evidence that I am morally obligated to ϕ, and the disjunction, rather than r alone, only counts as a reason, if it does, because it is only it, and not r, that is supported by Nguyen's evidence. But no plausible Objectivism about moral wrongness will also be non-Objectivist about obligating reasons. And that's just to say that an appeal to this conception of reasons as part of one's defense of an argument against Objectivism begs the question against Objectivism. So, contra Lord, one needn't grant that for one to be morally obligated to ϕ, one must be able to nonaccidentally ϕ for the reasons that make one's ϕing morally obligatory. And so it needn't be the case that RRAC is true.

Lord's Argument against Objectivism rests on RRAC. But RRAC is unmotivated, and so it gives us no grounds for rejecting Objectivism.[17]

3.4 The Jackson-Case Argument against Objectivism

More promising as an argument against Objectivism is one offered by Jackson (1991) and championed more recently by Zimmerman (2006, 2008). The argument begins with the following case:

---

[17] In yet more recent work, Lord (2018) offers a slightly altered version of this argument. He attempts to motivate the first premise of this slightly altered version of the argument by way of the following principle:

Link: When A is required to ϕ by the members of some set of reasons S, A is creditworthy for ϕing just in case A ϕs because of the members of some subset of S that are sufficiently strong to require A to ϕ.

Link, however, is subject to counterexample. Consider the following case: Z is Y's sixteen-year-old child. X solemnly promises Y, on Y's deathbed, to take care of Z and, in particular, to pay for Z's college costs. When Z reaches college age, at significant cost to herself, X pays Z's college costs, not because she promised Y to do so, but because it would benefit Z to pay for his college costs. In this case, X is required to pay for Z's college costs because of her solemn promise to Y to do so. Even so, however, her paying Z's college costs is most certainly a creditworthy act even though she doesn't do it because of any set of reasons sufficiently strong to require her doing so. The reasons for which she does pay Z's college costs – viz., that doing so would benefit Z – are not sufficiently strong to require her paying his college costs – this can be seen by noting that for any other party, W, whose college costs X is not promise-bound to pay, though it would benefit W for X to pay W's college costs, that fact doesn't require X to pay W's college costs.

Doctor: Doctor has a patient, Patient, who has a severely painful condition. In front of her are three medicines she could give to Patient. Doctor knows that medicine B will partially cure Patient, such that after administering it Patient will only suffer from an easily bearable, mild pain. Doctor also knows that one of medicine A and medicine C is a complete cure, such that after administering it Patient will suffer no pain, and the other is a lethal poison, such that after administering it Patient will die. Though medicine A is the complete cure and medicine C is the lethal poison, Doctor does not know, nor does she have any evidence concerning, which is which.

Doctor has four options:

NOTHING: do nothing, thereby allowing Patient's severe pain to persist
GIVE A: administer medicine A to Patient
GIVE B: administer medicine B to Patient
GIVE C: administer medicine C to Patient

In this case, it seems intuitive that Doctor ought to GIVE B and that insofar as Doctor is morally conscientious she will GIVE B. But doing GIVE B is to do what is, and what Doctor knows at the time of action to be, morally wrong according to Objectivism. According to Objectivism, the only morally permissible option for Doctor is GIVE A, and that's because only medicine A will in fact cure Patient's condition completely, and Doctor is morally obliged to do the best she can for Patient. If that's right, then it may seem that the notion of wrongness of ultimate concern to the morally conscientious person in their deliberations about what to do can't be the objective notion of wrongness. Because, if Doctor is morally conscientious, she most certainly will do what she knows any plausible objective moral theory would dictate that it would be morally wrong for her to do, the Objectivist's notion of wrongness can't be the notion of wrongness that the morally conscientious agent is ultimately concerned with in their deliberations about what to do. If Doctor is concerned to avoid acting wrongly, then, it seems, it is not objective wrongness that she is seeking to avoid.

This argument is stronger than the one that consists in a direct appeal to the intuition that it would not be morally wrong for Chen to flip the switch in *Switch*. That's because it purports to show that Objectivism entails that one can conscientiously do what one knows to be wrong as one does it. And that, it is deemed, is implausible. In *Switch* the Objectivist needn't deny that Chen can be morally conscientious when she flips the switch because in *Switch* Chen is acting in ignorance of the fact that flipping the switch will have the disastrous consequences that it does. From Chen's perspective, she is doing what Objectivism dictates she morally ought to do, for she is doing what she takes to be helping Gomez and harming no one. So, in *Switch* acting morally conscientiously needn't allow that one might do what one knows to be morally wrong as one does it. So, *Switch* needn't indicate that the morally conscientious person's concern is not to avoid acting objectively wrongly; it is plausible that Chen's being morally conscientious might still involve wanting to avoid acting objectively morally wrongly even when, because of her ignorance, she does what is in fact objectively morally wrong. But because Doctor's being morally conscientious requires her to do what she knows to be objectively morally wrong in *Doctor*, that does seem to put pressure on the thought that it is the Objectivist's notion of wrongness that the morally conscientious person is concerned to avoid when in their deliberations about what to do they try not to act wrongly.

3.4.1 A Reply to the Jackson-Case Argument

This Jackson-style argument against Objectivism is, arguably, the most potent anti-Objectivist argument currently in play.[18] It is not uncontroversial, however. It has been challenged. A crucial premise of the argument is that one can't morally conscientiously do what one knows to be wrong in the sense of "wrong" with which one in being morally conscientious is concerned not so to act. If it were possible for one to morally conscientiously do what one knew to be morally wrong in the sense of "wrong" with which one in being morally conscientious is ultimately concerned to avoid doing, then it wouldn't follow from the facts that the only morally conscientious thing to do in *Doctor* is GIVE B and that Doctor's doing GIVE B would be her doing something that she knows is morally wrong according to the Objectivist's notion of wrongness that that notion of wrongness is not the notion of wrongness at the heart of the morally conscientious person's ultimate concern not to act wrongly. It has been contended (by Bykvist 2009 and Graham 2010), however, that a morally conscientious person could well do what they know to be morally wrong when they do it and so the inference at the core of the Jackson-style argument against Objectivism is invalid.

But how could it be the case that a morally conscientious person might do what they know when they do it to be morally wrong, according to the notion of wrongness at play in their ultimate concern not to act wrongly? To see how, we need first to look a little more closely at the morally conscientious person's concern not to act wrongly. The morally conscientious person's concern not to act wrongly is not binary; that is, it is not the case that their concern is simply to not act wrongly. Because wrongness can come in degrees, the morally

---

[18] Kiesewetter (2017) offers a version of the Jackson-style argument, which he calls the Misguidance Argument, against Objectivism about what he calls "the deliberative 'ought'."

conscientious person's concern not to act wrongly is degreed in step with the various degrees of wrongness that their actions might have: they will be more concerned not to act very seriously wrongly than they will be not to act minorly wrongly. This fact, that the morally conscientious person's concern not to act wrongly is calibrated to the various believed degrees of wrongness of their potential actions, helps explain how it could be that a morally conscientious person might do what they know to be morally wrong when they do it.

First, a few words about degrees of moral wrongness. That there are degrees of moral wrongness seems intuitively quite plausible.[19] Not only can an agent do something morally wrong, but of two actions an agent can perform, one can be *more* morally wrong than another. This degreed notion of moral wrongness manifests itself both in intra-case and inter-case moral wrongness comparisons. Take first an intra-case comparison: Hussein is choosing between (a) doing nothing, (b) punching Chang in the stomach, and (c) stabbing Chang in the eye. Not only would taking either option (b) or option (c) be morally wrong, but taking (c) would be more morally wrong than would taking (b). Now take an inter-case comparison: on Monday Nguyen, instead of doing nothing, chooses to punch Lopez in the stomach, and on Tuesday she, instead of doing nothing, chooses to stab Lopez in the eye. Nguyen's punching of Lopez on Monday and her stabbing him on Tuesday were both morally wrong, but her stabbing him on Tuesday was more wrong than was her punching him on Monday. In both intra- and inter-case comparisons, then, two morally wrong actions can be compared to each other with respect to how wrong each is.

(A couple further points about degree of wrongness comparisons. First, though the examples to which I appeal all involve consequentialist consider-ations – the reason why stabbing someone in the eye is more morally wrong than is punching them in the stomach is quite clearly that the consequence of having one's eye stabbed is worse than that of having one's stomach punched – degree of wrongness comparisons needn't be grounded solely in consequentialist considerations. Mbeki's cheating on his spouse behind her back would be more morally wrong than would be his pinching her, and that would be true even if the consequences of his cheating, because she never found out about it, weren't particularly bad. Second, though it is of course quite plausible that coming up with exact numerical assignments to the various degrees of wrong-ness being compared is beyond our epistemic capacities, it seems, in principle, that this should be doable. Not only would Mbeki's cheating on his spouse be more wrong than would be his pinching her, but his cheating would be clearly

---

[19] Hurka (2019) offers an in-depth account of degrees of moral wrongness. Hurka talks of degrees of the *seriousness* of a wrong, and not of degrees of wrongness *per se*, but much of what he says can be understood in terms of degrees of wrongness themselves.

more than twice as wrong as his pinching her would be. So, though ordinal comparisons of degrees of wrongness are clearly possible, so too, it seems, should be cardinal comparisons.)

But how does recognizing both that there are degrees of moral wrongness and that the morally conscientious person's concern not to act wrongly is sensitive to them explain how it could be that a morally conscientious person might do what they know to be morally wrong? Well, if a morally conscientious person ever found themself in a situation in which they didn't know which of their options was morally permissible, but they did know that taking a chance at doing what is morally permissible would risk them doing something they knew to be very seriously morally wrong, they might opt instead to do something they knew was minorly morally wrong rather than take a chance at trying to do what is permissible, thereby taking a risk at doing something very seriously wrong. From the Objectivist standpoint, this is in fact exactly the situation that Doctor finds herself in in *Doctor*. She knows that completely curing Patient is the only morally permissible thing to do, but trying to do that, by doing one of GIVE A and GIVE C, would be to risk doing something very seriously morally wrong; viz., killing Patient. So, if she is morally conscientious, Doctor will GIVE B in *Doctor*, knowing that she is doing something minorly morally wrong in doing so – because she's not completely curing Patient – in order to avoid taking a risk at doing something very majorly morally wrong.

This isn't an argument for Objectivism. Rather, it is a defense of Objectivism against the Jackson-style argument against it. It appeals to a particular conception of moral conscientiousness that is at odds with a presupposition of the *Doctor*-based argument; viz., that, necessarily, a morally conscientious person will never do what they know to be morally wrong. So, whether the Jackson-style argument against Objectivism has any force, it turns out, depends on which conception of moral conscientiousness is more plausible. If the conception implicitly appealed to in the argument is more plausible than the Objectivist's alternative, then the Objectivist's reply will fall flat. If, on the other hand, the Objectivism-friendly conception of moral conscientiousness is more plausible, then the argument against Objectivism fails. A closer look at the competing conceptions of moral conscientiousness is called for.

3.4.2 Evaluating Competing Conceptions of Moral Conscientiousness

Consider first the conception of moral conscientiousness implicitly appealed to in the Jackson-style argument against Objectivism. According to this conception, the following is true:

No Deliberate Conscientious Wrongdoing: Necessarily, if S deliberately ϕs at t_1 and S believes at t_1 that their ϕing at t_1 is morally wrong, then it is not the case that S is being morally conscientious in ϕing at t_1.

What does *No Deliberate Conscientious Wrongdoing* have going for it? Well, it does seem undeniable that moral conscientiousness involves an aversion to acting wrongly, and *No Deliberate Conscientious Wrongdoing* is a simple and straightforward articulation of that aversion. There thus is indeed some intuitive force behind *No Deliberate Conscientious Wrongdoing*.

But, as we've seen, *No Deliberate Conscientious Wrongdoing* is not the only way to understand the morally conscientious person's aversion to acting morally wrongly. What's more, insofar as there are indeed degrees of moral wrongness, or, more simply, insofar as a morally conscientious person might believe that there are degrees of moral wrongness, a more nuanced articulation of the morally conscientious person's aversion to acting morally wrongly might be needed. According to the Objectivism-friendly conception of moral conscientiousness, instead of *No Deliberate Conscientious Wrongdoing*, the following is true:

Conscientiousness as a Degreed Concern about Wrongness: Necessarily, if S believes that S's ϕing would be, or lead to, them acting more seriously wrongly than would S's ψing, then if S is morally conscientious, S is more averse to ϕing than to ψing.

It follows from *Conscientiousness as a Degreed Concern about Wrongness* that believing an action is morally wrong entails having some aversion to doing it, but it also incorporates a sensitivity to degrees of wrongness. Insofar as there are indeed degrees of wrongness and *Conscientiousness as a Degreed Concern about Wrongness* incorporates a sensitivity to them whereas *No Deliberate Conscientious Wrongdoing* does not, that, in and of itself, might be a reason to prefer *Conscientiousness as a Degreed Concern about Wrongness* to *No Deliberate Conscientious Wrongdoing*.

What's more, there may be independent reasons to reject *No Deliberate Conscientious Wrongdoing*. Before explaining what those independent reasons are, however, I'll first explain and set aside another tempting, though, in the end, I think, bad objection to it. One might doubt *No Deliberate Conscientious Wrongdoing* on the grounds that it implausibly ties moral conscientiousness to *de dicto* beliefs about wrongness. Surely, you might think, one can be morally conscientious without having any particular beliefs about moral wrongness. (Or even, it might seem that one could be morally conscientious while believing that one was acting morally wrongly in doing what one does – as Huckleberry Finn does when he refuses to return Jim, the slave whom he has helped escape, back to his "master".) I don't think this works as an argument against *No Deliberate Conscientious Wrongdoing*, for though it is clear that one can act morally rightly, morally praiseworthily, and in a manner that demonstrates the goodness of one's character without having any *de dicto* beliefs about moral wrongness, it isn't clear that one can truly count as being morally conscientious without being punctiliously and fastidiously concerned about the moral permissibility of what one does. Being morally conscientious is distinct from being a good person; what these cases show is that one can indeed be a good person, and act in a way that shows that one is sensitive to moral considerations, without counting as morally conscientious. (Whereas Huckleberry Finn does demonstrate a goodness of character in not returning Jim to his "master," given that he thinks he is acting morally wrongly in doing so, it doesn't seem correct to call him particularly morally conscientious.) What's more, one can surely count as morally conscientious while at the same time being a morally bad person if, in particular, one has radically mistaken views about moral matters. (The morally conscientious Nazi, though probably not actual, is not a contradiction in terms.) Being morally conscientious, what's more, is not as morally important as being a good person is: were one to face a choice of either being a morally conscientious person or being a good person, one should most certainly choose the latter. So, I don't think that the fact that one can be a morally good person without having any *de dicto* beliefs about moral wrongness gives us good grounds to reject *No Deliberate Conscientious Wrongdoing*.

Here, however, I think, are better grounds for rejecting *No Deliberate Conscientious Wrongdoing*. If *No Deliberate Conscientious Wrongdoing* is true, it turns out that a person's being morally conscientious is inconsistent with their holding certain philosophical views. But, arguably, it is implausible that the mere holding of these philosophical views could, all on their own, render one not morally conscientious. What philosophical views are such that holding them is inconsistent with moral conscientiousness if *No Deliberate Conscientious Wrongdoing* is true? They are the view that moral wrongness dilemmas are possible and the view that Possibilism about moral wrongness is true. Next, I explain how it is that if *No Deliberate Conscientious Wrongdoing* is true, merely holding one of these philosophical views, all on its own, renders one not morally conscientious.[20]

---

[20] Note, the claim is not that the mere holding of a philosophical view can't make one not morally conscientious. Perhaps, certain reprehensible – racist, sexist, etc. – philosophical views might be such that the mere holding of them makes one not morally conscientious. The claim is that the mere holding of the particular views I shall consider – that moral wrongness dilemmas are possible, and that Possibilism about moral wrongness is true – cannot, in and of themselves, render one not morally conscientious.

The view that moral wrongness dilemmas are metaphysically possible is the view that it is metaphysically possible that one finds oneself in a situation in which all of one's options are morally wrong; that is, a situation in which no matter what one does, one acts morally wrongly. Here's an example of the kind of case that convinces some that moral wrongness dilemmas are in fact metaphysically possible:

> ***Bomb***: Terrorist has planted a bomb that will go off, killing 500 innocent people, unless FBI Agent can get Terrorist to tell him where the bomb is. If FBI Agent gets Terrorist to tell him where the bomb is, he will be able to locate and defuse the bomb before it goes off. The only thing FBI Agent can do to get Terrorist to tell him where the bomb is is to torture Terrorist's daughter.

> FBI Agent has two options:

> TORTURE: torture Terrorist's daughter, thereby finding out where the bomb is, defusing it, and saving the lives of the 500 innocent people

> ~TORTURE: not torture Terrorist's daughter, thereby allowing the 500 innocent people to be killed

Proponents of the metaphysical possibility of moral wrongness dilemmas point to cases like *Bomb* as one source of support for their view. Clearly the situation in *Bomb* is metaphysically possible. But, even so, both of FBI Agent's options seem morally wrong: TORTURE intuitively seems wrong because it is morally wrong to torture an innocent person even if doing so is necessary to save the lives of yet other innocent people, and ~TORTURE intuitively seems wrong because it's morally wrong to let 500 innocent people be killed if one can easily prevent it without causing nearly as much harm. Note, it's not just that both options will involve bad consequences – they will – and so, no matter what FBI Agent does, he will have done something bad. That might well be true in a situation in which both options are morally permissible. Rather, it's that, according to the proponent of the metaphysical possibility of moral wrongness dilemmas, no matter what FBI Agent does, he acts morally wrongly; that is, he acts in a way that is forbidden by morality. Whether moral wrongness dilemmas are metaphysically possible is a very contentious issue in normative ethics. Many think that moral wrongness dilemmas are impossible because they flout principles of deontic logic. Others, on the other hand, think that the principles of deontic logic inconsistent with the possibility of moral wrongness dilemmas are themselves false (and shown to be so by the metaphysical possibility of moral wrongness dilemmas!).[21]

---

[21] For more on the moral dilemmas literature, see Gowans (1987), Sinnott-Armstrong (1988), and Mason (1996).

Now, as I say, whether moral wrongness dilemmas are in fact metaphysically possible is quite controversial. But what isn't controversial is that it is metaphysically possible that there be people who believe that such dilemmas are metaphysically possible. There actually are people who believe in the metaphysical possibility of moral wrongness dilemmas, and so such people are, of course, metaphysically possible. However, if *No Deliberate Conscientious Wrongdoing* is true, then none of these people is morally conscientious. How so? Well, because it is also metaphysically possible for a believer in the possibility of moral wrongness dilemmas to find themselves in a situation that they believe to be an actual moral wrongness dilemma, it follows from *No Deliberate Conscientious Wrongdoing* that such a person is disposed to deliberately and knowingly act in a way they believe to be morally wrong in such a situation. For instance, a believer in the metaphysical possibility of moral wrongness dilemmas might well be disposed to ~TORTURE while at the same time believing that doing so would be morally wrong were they ever to find themselves in the situation FBI Agent finds himself in in *Bomb*. But being disposed to ~TORTURE in *Bomb* while at the same time believing that it is morally wrong to ~TORTURE along with *No Deliberate Conscientious Wrongdoing* entails that were they to find themselves in *Bomb*, they wouldn't be morally conscientious. And, as it is arguable that one doesn't count as morally conscientious unless one is disposed to behave morally conscientiously in whatever situation one might find oneself, it follows that one's mere holding of the belief that moral wrongness dilemmas are metaphysically possible is enough to render one, whether one ever finds oneself in a situation like *Bomb* or not, not morally conscientious.[22] But that's implausible.

Zimmerman (2014), the main defender of *No Deliberate Conscientious Wrongdoing*, bites this bullet. He responds to this objection by noting that though a person who is generally morally conscientious might find themselves in a situation that they take to be a moral wrongness dilemma, were they to truly believe that of their situation, they couldn't then act morally conscientiously in their situation. This is simply to deny what seems intuitive, namely that merely

---

[22] What if they aren't disposed to do anything knowingly and deliberately in a situation they take to be a moral dilemma because they are disposed to do whatever they do nondeliberately? Perhaps that's in fact what we should say about morally conscientious agents who believe in the possibility of moral dilemmas; viz., that were they to find themselves in such a situation, because of its dilemmatic nature they wouldn't end up deliberately doing what they in fact would end up doing, and would instead do what they do either akratically or in some other nondeliberate way. If this is right, then this argument based on the possibility of morally conscientious people who believe in the possibility of moral dilemmas may not work. However, the variation on it I discuss below, based on the possibility of a person who believes in the possibility of moral dilemmas, some of the options of which are more wrong than others, should go through just as well. Thanks to Doug Portmore for helpful discussion on this point.

finding oneself in a situation one takes to be a moral wrongness dilemma doesn't entail all on its own that one doesn't act morally conscientiously. What's more, Zimmerman is mistaken if he thinks that someone who is in general morally conscientious only becomes unconscientious once they find themself in a situation they take to be a moral wrongness dilemma, for that overlooks the point, made earlier, that if they are disposed to act wrongly in the situation they take to be a moral wrongness dilemma, that in itself renders them not morally conscientious *tout court*, even if they never do find themself in what they take to be a moral wrongness dilemma.

Not only is Zimmerman's response the biting of a nasty bullet, but the screws might be tightened even further. Not only might one believe one is in a moral wrongness dilemma, one might also think that of one's various morally wrong options in such a situation, certain ones are *more seriously wrong* than are others. And if one did believe one was in a moral wrongness dilemma in which one believed of one of one's options that it was least wrong, were one morally conscientious, one would take that option instead of any of the rest. In fact, how are we to characterize the comparison between the agent who takes what they believe is the least wrong option and the agent who takes what they believe is the more wrong one, in such circumstances? It seems that the only metric it makes sense to employ here is one of moral conscientiousness. The agent in what they take to be a moral wrongness dilemma who takes what they believe is the least wrong option is acting more morally conscientiously than is the agent who, in what they take to be a moral wrongness dilemma, takes an option they believe to be more wrong than some other option of which they believe it is less wrong.[23] Taking what one believes is the least wrong option, if there is one and one knows which it is, when in what one takes to be a moral wrongness dilemma is the morally conscientious thing to do, after all. And so, plausibly, were one to find oneself in such a situation, that is what moral conscientiousness would dictate one do. If that's right, then, Zimmerman's bullet biting notwithstanding, *No Deliberate Conscientious Wrongdoing* is false.

The same kind of argument against *No Deliberate Conscientious Wrongdoing* could be run with a different philosophical belief, one that takes a stand on another contentious debate in normative ethics: that between Actualists and Possibilists about moral wrongness. Actualists maintain, and Possibilists deny, that a person's potential future voluntary behavior – what they

---

[23] I guess it might be open to Zimmerman to claim that the one agent acts more morally conscientiously than the other even though the former doesn't act morally conscientiously (just as X can be taller than Y without X's being tall). But why say that? Why not instead say that acting morally conscientiously entails taking one of the options one has of which one believes that it is least wrong?

will later do *were* they to do some particular thing now – is relevant to the moral status of what they presently do. As with the Subjectivism/Objectivism debate, an example will help illustrate what's in dispute between Actualists and Possibilists:

> **Headache**: On Monday, Patient has an excruciating headache. Though it will go away on its own in five hours, drug D will cure it immediately. However, as D is a very potent drug, if it is administered on Monday, drug E must be administered on Tuesday in order to counter its side effects, otherwise Patient will die. Doctor can administer D on Monday, but she knows that if she does so, even though she will be able to administer E on Tuesday, because of her own laziness then, she won't.

> Doctor has two options on Monday:

> GIVE D: administer D to Patient
> ~GIVE D: not administer D to Patient

Possibilists contend that it would be morally wrong for Doctor to ~GIVE D on Monday. Actualists maintain not only that it would not be morally wrong for Doctor to ~GIVE D on Monday but also that it would be morally wrong for Doctor to GIVE D. The Actualist points out that Doctor's administering D to Patient on Monday would have disastrous consequences – Patient will die on Tuesday if Doctor administers D on Monday. The Possibilist counters that it would be morally wrong for Doctor not to do the best she can for Patient and there is a course of action completely open to her – administer D on Monday and then administer E on Tuesday – in which she cures Patient without killing her.[24]

Now, just as a person can believe the true moral theory, whatever it happens to be, and be morally conscientious in *Doctor*, so too can a person believe Possibilism and be morally conscientious in *Headache*. However, I take it to be clear that acting morally conscientiously in *Headache* entails doing ~GIVE D. And according to the Possibilist, doing ~GIVE D is morally wrong in *Headache*. But if that's right, then **No Deliberate Conscientious Wrongdoing** is false: though a Possibilist will believe that doing ~GIVE D is morally wrong, nevertheless, they can be morally conscientious and deliberately ~GIVE D in *Headache*. In fact, as both Actualists and Possibilists should equally agree, the only way for Doctor to be morally conscientious on Monday in *Headache* is for her to ~GIVE D: given her knowledge that Patient will die if she does GIVE D,

---

[24] Actualists include Goldman (1976), Sobel (1976), Jackson and Pargetter (1986), Goble (1993), Portmore (2011), and Ross (2012). Possibilists include Goldman (1978), Greenspan (1978), Thomason (1981), Feldman (1986), Zimmerman (1996, 2008), Vessel (2009), Vorobej (2000), Cohen and Timmerman (2016), and Graham (2019).

the only morally conscientious thing for Doctor to do on Monday is ~GIVE D.[25] And so, *No Deliberate Conscientious Wrongdoing* is false. The only way around this argument is to declare Possibilism conceptually incoherent. But Possibilism is not conceptually incoherent.

3.4.3 In Support of Conscientiousness as a Degreed Concern about Wrongness

Not only can *No Deliberate Conscientious Wrongdoing* be cast into doubt. More can be said in favor of *Conscientiousness as a Degreed Concern about Wrongness* as well. The degreed concern not to act wrongly that is at the core of moral conscientiousness according to *Conscientiousness as a Degreed Concern about Wrongness* can be seen in a number of ways. First, a morally conscientious person's preferences and conditional dispositions will match the degrees of wrongness of their options. If a morally conscientious agent faces a choice between (a) doing nothing, (b) slapping an innocent person in the face, and (c) stabbing another innocent person in the eye, not only will they prefer (a) to both (b) and (c), they will prefer (b) to (c). And not only will they be disposed to do (a) in such a scenario, they will be disposed *to do (b) if they do not do (a)*. According to *No Deliberate Conscientious Wrongdoing*, these features of the morally conscientious agent are inexplicable – for being concerned not to knowingly and deliberately act wrongly entails nothing on its own about having preferences among morally wrong options, nor does it entail anything about one's conditional dispositions to act wrongly given that one does not act rightly.

The morally conscientious person's greater concern not to act more seriously wrongly rather than to act less seriously wrongly can also be seen in how they behave in light of knowledge of their own potential future unconscientiousness. Consider the following scenario:

---

[25] It might seem odd to think that Doctor can be morally conscientious in *Headache*, given that she knows that were she to GIVE D on Monday she would lazily fail to administer E on Tuesday. If she were morally conscientious, wouldn't she GIVE D and then not lazily fail to administer E on Tuesday? True. She would do that were she morally conscientious *from Monday all the way through Tuesday*. But the question Doctor faces in *Headache* is what to do given that she knows that she will lazily fail to administer E on Tuesday were she to GIVE D on Monday. What this means is that she knows on Monday that if she were to GIVE D on Monday, she would not be morally conscientious from Monday all the way through Tuesday. That she will lazily fail to administer E on Tuesday if she does GIVE D on Monday shows that were she to GIVE D on Monday, she would fail to be morally conscientious on Tuesday. But it doesn't follow from that that she can't be morally conscientious on Monday. In asking what it would be morally conscientious for her to do on Monday, we're asking the question what would it be morally conscientious for her to do given her knowledge of her own potential future moral unconscientiousness. What I claim should be common ground between Actualists and Possibilists is that the only morally conscientious thing for Doctor to do on Monday, given her knowledge of her own potential future moral unconscientiousness on Tuesday, is to ~GIVE D.

House: Nguyen stands at the front door of a house. She knows that if she enters the house at t_1, she will go on to voluntarily kill an innocent person, Torres, at t_2 (i.e., she will go on to kill Torres at t_2, while at t_2 being able to not kill him then). She also knows that if she does not enter the house at t_1 she will go on to voluntarily punch an innocent person, Chen, in the stomach at t_2 (i.e., she will go on to punch Chen in the stomach at t_2, while at t_2 being able to not punch him then).

Nguyen has two options at t_1:

ENTER: enter the house (in which case she will then go on to voluntarily kill Torres)

~ENTER: not enter the house (in which case she will then go on to voluntarily punch Chen in the stomach)

Even though ENTER and ~ENTER are both morally permissible for Nguyen in this scenario,[26] if she is morally conscientious at t_1, Nguyen will ~ENTER at t_1. The explanation of why, if she is morally conscientious at t_1, Nguyen will ~ENTER is that, even though no matter what she does at t_1 she will act wrongly at t_2 – both killing Torres at t_2 after doing ENTER and punching Chen in the stomach at t_2 after doing ~ENTER are morally wrong – were she to ENTER, she would act *more* wrongly at t_2 than she would were she to ~ENTER. Here again the morally conscientious agent's degreed concern with not acting wrongly manifests itself.

In fact, in *House* not only do we find support for **Conscientiousness as a Degreed Concern about Wrongness**, we also find another argument against **No Deliberate Conscientious Wrongdoing**. **No Deliberate Conscientious Wrongdoing** leaves completely unexplained the datum that necessarily, if Nguyen is morally conscientious at t_1 in *House*, she will ~ENTER. As both ENTER and ~ENTER are morally permissible, there is nothing in **No Deliberate Conscientious Wrongdoing** that explains why Nguyen, if she is morally conscientious, will take ~ENTER. What's more, a proponent of **No Deliberate Conscientious Wrongdoing** can't appeal to the morally conscientious agent's future-directed binary concern not to act wrongly to explain why, if she is morally conscientious, Nguyen will ~ENTER, for no matter what she does at t_1 she will act wrongly at t_2. We need to appeal to the morally conscientious person's degreed concern not to act wrongly – a concern that concerns not just avoiding acting wrongly at the moment but also not acting wrongly in the future – in order to explain why Nguyen's moral conscientiousness entails that she will ~ENTER at t_1 in *House*. It is precisely because she wants more to not

---

[26] I'm here assuming that Possibilism is true. Because she will be able to refrain from harming anyone at t_2 whether she enters the building or not, both ENTER and ~ENTER are morally permissible for her.

act seriously morally wrongly than she does to not act less seriously morally wrongly in the future that a morally conscientious Nguyen will ~ENTER at t_1 in *House*. **Conscientiousness as a Degreed Concern about Wrongness** can account for this. **No Deliberate Conscientious Wrongdoing** cannot.[27]

Now one might protest on behalf of **No Deliberate Conscientious Wrongdoing** that it is consistent with it that a morally conscientious person might be more concerned not to do seriously morally wrong things than they are to not do less seriously morally wrong things. **No Deliberate Conscientious Wrongdoing** is only a necessary condition on moral conscientiousness, after all. Perhaps one might claim that both **No Deliberate Conscientious Wrongdoing** and **Conscientiousness as a Degreed Concern about Wrongness** are true. There are two problems with this reply. First, as was argued earlier, there are independent grounds for thinking that **No Deliberate Conscientious Wrongdoing** is false. And second, **No Deliberate Conscientious Wrongdoing** and **Conscientiousness as a Degreed Concern about Wrongness** are in tension with each other. Accepting **Conscientiousness as a Degreed Concern about Wrongness** puts pressure on **No Deliberate Conscientious Wrongdoing**. Once one accepts **Conscientiousness as a Degreed Concern about Wrongness**, it becomes clear that there might well be cases in which a morally conscientious person would do what they know to be morally wrong – in particular, they will do so if in doing so they can avoid taking a chance at doing something very seriously morally wrong. And this is because their greater concern not to do what is seriously morally wrong will outweigh their concern not to do what is much less seriously wrong and motivate them to do the less seriously morally

---

[27] Zimmerman might contest the claim that his understanding of moral conscientiousness is unable to account for the data concerning what a morally conscientious agent would do in *House* and prefer and be conditionally disposed to do in cases where one has more than one morally wrong option, and, in particular, in cases in which one believes one has a more seriously wrong and a less seriously wrong option. He might note that his conception of the morally conscientious agent might well include a commitment to maximizing what he calls "actual deontic value" when one knows how to. Actual deontic value is supposed to be a cardinalization of the moral ranking of options (ranking in terms of what, though?) that the true moral theory, whatever it happens to be, assigns to one's options. And perhaps these preferences and conditional dispositions to behave of the morally conscientious person might be explained by the morally conscientious person's concern to maximize actual deontic value. The problem with this reply is twofold. First, there is nothing inherent in moral conscientiousness that is maximizing. Rather, moral conscientiousness is a matter of being concerned to avoid acting wrongly. Second, and more importantly, "actual deontic value" is a philosopher's construct. It has, and need have, no place in the conceptual repertoire of a morally conscientious agent. Whereas it is true that one couldn't possibly count as being morally conscientious without possessing the concept of moral wrongness (and in particular, I would argue, a concept of moral wrongness that admits of degrees), one most certainly can be morally conscientious without possessing the concept of actual deontic value at all. Thus, as one needn't even have the concept of actual deontic value, maximizing actual deontic value can't be at the core of the concern that makes a morally conscientious person morally conscientious.

wrong thing. As noted earlier, this, one might think, is precisely what is going on in *Doctor*. In *Doctor*, if Doctor is morally conscientious, she will GIVE B precisely because doing so is the only way she can avoid taking a risk of acting seriously morally wrongly – if she does either GIVE A or GIVE C, she will risk acting very seriously morally wrongly, because one of them is a lethal poison and if she gives that to Patient, he will die; and if she does NOTHING then she clearly acts more wrongly than she does in doing GIVE B because doing GIVE B relieves most of Patient's suffering whereas doing NOTHING leaves Patient in severe pain. The moral data in *Doctor* seem compatible with *Conscientiousness as a Degreed Concern about Wrongness* and there are serious concerns with *No Deliberate Conscientious Wrongdoing*. All of this might suggest that the Objectivist-friendly conception of moral conscientiousness (according to which *Conscientiousness as a Degreed Concern about Wrongness* is true but *No Deliberate Conscientious Wrongdoing* is false) is preferable to that implicitly appealed to in the Jackson-style argument against Objectivism (according to which *No Deliberate Conscientious Wrongdoing* is true). And if that's right, then the Jackson-style argument does not refute Objectivism.

3.5 The Conditionalization Argument against Objectivism

I now consider another argument against Objectivism about moral wrongness. According to this argument, the fact that agents have certain first-order normative powers shows Objectivism to be false. In particular, the argument crucially relies on the fact that in making promises and giving our consent to others we can conditionalize these things not only on features of the world outside of us, but also on our own and others' subjective circumstances at the time of action. For example, consider the following two cases:

Conditional Promise: Khan has a patient, Hussein, suffering from mild chronic pain. Khan promises Hussein that if she, Khan, believes of a treatment that it has a significant risk of making him lose his hair, she will not prescribe it. Khan believes that treatment T might cure Hussein's chronic pain, and she believes that it has a significant risk of making Hussein lose his hair. T will in fact not cure Hussein's condition and there is in fact no risk whatsoever of T's making Hussein lose his hair. Khan prescribes T and Hussein, with his full head of hair, continues to suffer mild chronic pain.

Conditional Consent: Lopez tells Mbeki, who doesn't own a car and to whom Lopez has given her spare set of car keys, that if ever he, Mbeki, believes that he may significantly benefit himself by using her car, then he may use it. Mbeki believes, in accord with his evidence, that if he drives into town he will receive a prize of $10,000. In fact, Mbeki will not receive a prize of $10,000 if he drives into town. Mbeki drives into town using Lopez's car and disappointedly discovers that he has been duped. Because Mbeki has used her car, Lopez is unable to use it to pick her friend up from the airport.

I take it to be clear that in *Conditional Promise* Khan acts morally wrongly in prescribing T for Hussein, and in *Conditional Consent* Mbeki does not act wrongly in using Lopez's car. True, Khan does not end up causing Hussein to lose his hair by prescribing treatment T, but because she believed that doing so was risky with respect to baldness and she promised not to prescribe any treatment she herself believed was risky with respect to baldness, she has morally wrongly broken her promise. What's more, Hussein has a legitimate moral complaint against Khan; in prescribing T while believing that it was risky with respect to baldness, Khan has violated the right Hussein has against her that she not prescribe a treatment that she believes is risky with respect to baldness, a right she gave Hussein in making the promise she made to him. And, turning to *Conditional Promise*, even though Mbeki uses Lopez's car, thereby preventing her from picking her friend up from the airport, his doing so is not morally wrong because the condition of Lopez's consent for him to use the car has been satisfied – he does believe that using it would benefit him significantly. Again, Lopez has no ground for complaint against Mbeki.

Because we can conditionalize our promises and our consent on anything whatsoever – I can, for instance, conditionalize my consent to your being on my land on Google's stock's reaching a certain price – we can conditionalize them on features of our own or others' subjective circumstances. And as *Conditional Promise* and *Conditional Consent* demonstrate, when we do so we can thereby render the moral status of an agent's action dependent on their own subjective circumstances. Khan's prescribing T is morally wrong, but had she not believed that T was risky with respect to baldness when she did so, her doing so would not have been morally wrong. And Mbeki's using of Lopez's car is not morally wrong because he believed that doing so would significantly benefit himself, but had he not believed this, his doing so would have been morally wrong. And so in *Conditional Promise* and *Conditional Consent* the moral status of Khan's and Mbeki's actions is grounded, at least partly, in their subjective circumstances. And so, so goes the argument, Objectivism about moral wrongness is false.[28]

---

[28] The *Conditional Promise*- and *Conditional Consent*-based arguments, if they work, establish that in some cases the moral status of an agent's action can be grounded in facts about the beliefs of the agent in question. Parallel arguments *mutatis mutandis* could be offered in an attempt to establish that in some cases (cases in which the promise or the consent is conditionalized on the agent's evidence) the moral status of an agent's action can be grounded in facts about the agent's evidence at the time of action.

The Objectivist may cry foul here. They might suggest that *Conditional Promise* and *Conditional Consent* do not show that the moral status of an agent's action is sometimes grounded in their subjective circumstances. What the wrongness of Khan's prescribing T is grounded in in *Conditional Promise*, they might argue, is the purely objective fact *that the condition of Khan's promise has been satisfied* in that case. And what the permissibility of Mbeki's using Lopez's car is grounded in in *Conditional Consent*, they might claim, is the purely objective fact *that the condition of Lopez's consent has been satisfied* in that case. In this way an Objectivist might object that *Conditional Promise* and *Conditional Consent* do not refute Objectivism.

Whether this reply to the *Conditional Promise-* and *Conditional Consent*-based arguments against Objectivism succeeds will depend crucially on how we understand the grounding involved in the definitions of Objectivism, Subjectivism, and Ecumenism. Why? Well, consider the following: though the moral fact, m, that Khan's prescribing T is wrong is partially grounded in the purely objective fact, f_1, that the condition of Khan's promise has been satisfied, that fact itself, plausibly, is at least partially grounded in Khan's subjective circumstances being what they are (it is partly *because* she believes of treatment T that it has a significant risk of making Hussein lose his hair that the condition of Khan's promise is satisfied in *Conditional Promise*), and Khan's subjective circumstances being what they are is a purely subjective fact, f_2. We thus have a chain of grounding here.

Chain: m is partially grounded in f_1, and f_1 is partially grounded in f_2

The Objectivist's reply to the *Conditional Promise-* and *Conditional Consent*-based arguments against it, then, will work only if either (1) the notion of grounding in the first conjunct of ***Chain*** is different from the notion of grounding in the second conjunct of ***Chain***, or (2) the notion of grounding in both conjuncts is not transitive. For if the notion of grounding in both conjuncts of ***Chain*** is the same and that notion of grounding is transitive, it will follow from ***Chain*** that m, the fact that Khan's prescribing T is wrong, is partially grounded (in the notion of grounding in terms of which Objectivism, Subjectivism, and Ecumenism are defined) in the subjective fact, f_2, that Khan's subjective circumstances are what they are. And that, if true, would suffice for the falsity of Objectivism and, thus, the *Conditional Promise*-based argument against Objectivism would succeed. And so, similarly, for the Objectivist reply to the *Conditional Consent*-based argument against Objectivism.

(A point about terminology: here I am allowing that an objective fact can be grounded, either fully or even partially, in a subjective fact. One might think, however, that the intuitive notions of "subjective fact" and "objective fact" are ones that preclude an objective fact ever being grounded, either fully or even partially, in a subjective fact. Because I define a person's subjective circumstances as that set of facts that consists in all and only the facts about how the world appears to them (i.e., a set of facts constituted either by facts about their beliefs, or about their evidence, etc.), on my definitions, it clearly is possible for an objective fact, like the fact that the condition of Khan's promise is satisfied, to be grounded in a subjective fact, like the fact that Khan believed that treatment T has a significant risk of making Hussein bald. If one instead held that no objective fact could be grounded, either fully or even partially, in a subjective fact, the response being considered here would scotch the Objectivist's reply even more resoundingly, for in that case, because the fact that the condition of Khan's promise is satisfied is partially grounded in the unquestionably subjective fact that Khan believed that treatment T has a significant risk of making Hussein bald, the fact that the condition of Khan's promise is satisfied would not count as an objective fact in the first place.)

Is the notion of grounding in the two conjuncts of *Chain* the same? And if so, is that notion of grounding transitive? These are difficult questions. A grounding pluralist, such as Fine (2012), according to whom there are different types of grounding, might claim that though the notion of grounding in the first conjunct of *Chain* is normative (as any grounding pluralist would also claim is the notion of grounding in play in the definitions of Objectivism, Subjectivism, and Ecumenism), the notion of grounding in the second conjunct of *Chain* is not. If so, then it wouldn't follow from *Chain* that m is normatively grounded in f_2 and thus that the *Conditional Promise*-based argument against Objectivism succeeds. If, on the other hand, a grounding monist, such as Berker (2018), is correct that there is one and only one true grounding relation, not multiple distinct ones, then if that relation is in fact transitive, as Berker takes it to be, then it would follow from *Chain* that m is normatively grounded in f_2 (because to be normatively grounded just is to be grounded *simpliciter*) and thus that the *Conditional Promise*-based argument against Objectivism succeeds. Now, settling the debate over grounding pluralism and over the transitivity of grounding relations is beyond the scope of this inquiry, but whether the *Conditional Promise*- and *Conditional Consent*-based arguments against Objectivism succeed hangs upon their resolution.[29]

---

[29] The assumption that grounding relations are transitive is one that is widely held in the grounding literature. For a canonical statement of the transitivity of grounding see Rosen (2010). Some have offered counterexamples against the transitivity of grounding (e.g., Schaffer 2012), but yet others have argued that the putative counterexamples fail (e.g., Litland 2013).

3.6 The Risky Rescue Argument against Objectivism

Another argument against Objectivism is also rooted in first-order normative considerations. In this case, the kind of case that puts pressure on strict Objectivism is that of potentially risky rescue:

> **Risky Rescue**: An innocent child lies unconscious in a room in which a bomb is about to go off. If the child is not carried out of the room, he will be killed in the explosion. There are two exits from the room, one of which, the left exit, is locked and the other of which, the right exit, is unlocked. If Nguyen enters the room to try to rescue the child by carrying him out of the room, she'll only have enough time to try leaving by one of the exits before the bomb goes off. If she enters, picks up the child, and then tries to leave by the locked exit, she, along with the child, will be killed in the explosion. Nguyen does not know, nor does her evidence indicate, which of the two exits is locked and which is unlocked. And she does know that were she to enter the room, once in the room, she still would not know, nor would her evidence then indicate, which of the two exits was unlocked. (She can't leave by the door through which she is able to enter the room because it will lock behind her after she enters the room.) If Nguyen does not enter the room, then though the child will be killed in the blast, Nguyen will remain unharmed.

I take it to be clear that it would not be morally wrong for Nguyen not to enter the room in this case. Because she does not know which of the exits is unlocked, even though there is a course of action she can perform – entering the room, picking up the child, and leaving by the right exit – such that were she to perform it she would save the child without suffering any harm at all, she is not morally obliged to save the child. However, were it the case that she knew which of the doors was unlocked, it would be morally wrong for her not to enter the room and save the child. So, the permissibility of her not entering the room in *Risky Rescue* is true partly in virtue of her subjective circumstances. Thus, Objectivism is false.

At this point, however, remembering the Objectivist's appeal to the distinction between wrongness and blameworthiness to defuse the *Switch*-based argument against it, you might well ask: why can't the Objectivist respond to the *Risky Rescue*-based argument against it by claiming that not entering the room is morally wrong, though blamelessly so? This won't work because not only is Nguyen's not entering the room blameless, it would also be perfectly consistent with her being morally conscientious for her not to enter the room. But that is inconsistent with a plausible principle about moral conscientiousness:

> **Conscientious Aversion to Wrongdoing**: Necessarily, a morally conscientious person would never refrain from ϕing at t_1 if they knew at t_1 (i) that ϕing is not morally wrong, (ii) that were they to refrain from ϕing, they would do

something wrong at t_1, and (iii) that it is not the case that were they to refrain from ϕing, they would act less wrongly overall at and after t_1 than they would were they to ϕ at t_1.[30]

This principle just falls out of the morally conscientious person's degreed concern to avoid acting wrongly in the future; intuitively, it says that if one knows that doing a certain thing now is not wrong, and one also knows that not doing that thing will lead to one's acting more wrongly overall than one would were one to do that thing now, then one will do that thing now. And it follows from this principle and the intuitive data in *Risky Rescue* that not entering the room is not an instance of blameless wrongdoing. Were not entering the room wrong, though blamelessly so, it would follow from **Conscientious Aversion to Wrongdoing** that Nguyen's being morally conscientious would entail her entering the room in *Risky Rescue* – because Nguyen would know (i) that entering the room is not morally wrong, (ii) that were she to refrain from entering the room, her doing so would be morally wrong, and (iii) that it is not the case that were she to refrain from entering the room, she would act less wrongly overall at and after t_1 than she would were she to enter the room – but Nguyen can be morally conscientious and not enter the room at t_1. Thus, Nguyen's not entering the room is not morally wrong. But it would be morally wrong if her subjective circumstances were otherwise; if, in particular, she knew at t_1, or perhaps her evidence at t_1 indicated, that she would know at t_2 which of the two exits was unlocked. So, that her not entering the room is not wrong is grounded, at least partly, in her subjective circumstances, and so Objectivism about moral wrongness is indeed false.

Though the Objectivist cannot resist the *Risky Rescue*-based argument by appealing to blameless wrongdoing, they might try to make a maneuver similar to that described earlier in their reply to the arguments against Objectivism based on *Conditional Promise* and *Conditional Consent*. An Objectivist might claim that though there clearly is a sense of "can perform" for which Nguyen certainly can perform the course of action that would end up saving herself and the child – she can, of course, enter the room, pick up the child, and exit via the right exit – there is just as clearly also a sense of "can perform" for which she cannot perform the course of action that would end up saving herself and the child – as she has no idea which of the left and right exits is the unlocked one, before entering the room she is not able to execute the course of action that would save the child and herself from being killed. What's more, you might think both that it is the latter sense of "can perform" that is immediately relevant

---

The third clause is necessary to accommodate the kinds of cases that split Actualists and Possibilists about moral wrongness.

to the moral status of her action and that whether she can perform the series of actions necessary to save the child and herself, in that sense of "can perform," is part of her objective circumstances. What a person can and cannot do are, after all, paradigmatic objective facts (they aren't *themselves* facts about how the world appears to one). And so, as the grounding of the permissibility of Nguyen's not rescuing the child is in an objective fact about her abilities, the argument against Objectivism fails.

This reply to the *Risky Rescue*-based argument against Objectivism, like the response to the *Conditional Promise*- and the *Conditional Consent*-based arguments, will, for exactly analogous reasons, hang on the issues concerning grounding considered earlier; viz., whether grounding pluralism is true and whether the relevant grounding relations are transitive. So, this argument against Objectivism, as well, is inconclusive.

These are some of the main arguments against Objectivism about moral wrongness. As we've seen, none of them is conclusive. Objectivism may be false, but none of these arguments definitively establishes that it is. The Brute Intuition Argument is only as strong as the intuition upon which it is based, the Action-Guiding/Usability Argument is underdeveloped, and Lord's Argument relies on premises that are not sufficiently motivated. The Jackson-Case Argument, though a stronger argument, depends for its cogency on a particular conception of moral conscientiousness, one that seems inferior to a more Objectivist-friendly conception, a conception that undermines a key premise in the argument. The Conditionalization Argument and the Risky Rescue Argument both rely on certain plausible first-order normative claims. Whether they work, however, depends on the status of certain controversial claims in the metaphysics of grounding, ones we are not here in a position to evaluate.

4 Against Subjectivism

I now turn to canvassing a number of different arguments against Subjectivism. The conclusion of this section is that, though a number of these arguments are at best inconclusive, some of them do seem to succeed in showing that strict Subjectivism is false.

4.1 Ross's Argument against Subjectivism

One argument against Subjectivism about moral wrongness is due to Ross (2002: 32). Ross writes:

> Many people would be inclined to say that the right act for me is not that whose general nature I have been describing, viz., that which if I were

omniscient I should see to be my duty, but that which on all the evidence available to me I should think to be my duty. But suppose that from the state of partial knowledge in which I think A to be my duty, I could pass to a state of perfect knowledge in which I saw act B to be my duty, should I not say "act B was the right act for me to do"?

When we change our mind about what we morally ought to do after investigating our situation and determining that the morally relevant factors are such and such rather than so and so, we come to think that what we've discovered to be what we morally ought to do is what we morally ought to have done all along. It's not as if in investigating our situation more fully we set out to change our moral situation. Rather, we're trying to figure out what our moral situation in fact is. If this seeming is veridical, then our moral obligations are not grounded in our evidence, or our beliefs, about our situation but rather in the objective facts of our situation, facts that through investigation we come to appreciate and through an appreciation of which come to know what our moral obligations both are and were prior to our investigation.

For example, suppose in *Doctor*, Doctor sets out to find out which of medicines A, B, and C is the perfect cure and discovers through her investigations that it is medicine A that is the perfect cure. Surely once she has discovered that medicine A is the perfect cure it would be morally wrong for her to do anything other than GIVE A. Because she'll think that any other course of action would be morally wrong to perform, Doctor will think that what she morally ought to do is GIVE A. But not only will she think that, she'll think that in discovering that what she morally ought to do is GIVE A, she'll think that she's discovered something that was true all along; viz., that what she morally ought to have done before investigating – that is, when she was in a state of ignorance about what she morally ought to do – was GIVE A. She'll think to herself: "It's good that I investigated and found out that what I morally ought to do is, and ought to have done was, administer A." If this thought is veridical, then it can't be that the moral status of her action is fully grounded in her subjective circumstances.

This argument against Subjectivism is not decisive. A proponent of Subjectivism can reject the intuitions around which this argument is based; that is, they can maintain that in finding out more about her situation, either Doctor won't think she's discovered what she ought to have done all along, or though she might think that, that thought would be mistaken. Why shouldn't a change in the agent's epistemic situation cause a change in their moral situation? After all, other changes in an agent's situation make changes in their moral situation – if, for instance, Doctor were given a fourth drug D and told that it would not only be a perfect cure for Patient but would also give Patient lots of pleasure, then surely what Doctor morally ought to do in that situation would be to give drug D and not whatever she was morally obligated to do prior to being given drug D. Acquiring a new drug can change the moral facts of a person's situation, and so too, you might think, does acquiring new evidence. So, when an agent acquires more information they do in fact change their moral situation from what it was, so might a Subjectivist say, and they thereby render the moral status of their various options other than what they were before their investigation.

Another attempt to press this line of argument against Subjectivism appeals to cases involving forgetting. Consider a version of *Doctor* in which Doctor, though she once knew which of medicines A and C was the perfect cure, has subsequently forgotten which is which. In such a situation, Doctor might plausibly think to herself, "I know that what I really morally ought to give Patient is one of A and C, because one of them is the perfect cure and that's the one I'm morally obliged to give him, but I've forgotten which one that is." If Doctor has such a thought and the thought is not mistaken, then that, once again, would put some pressure on Subjectivism. For if it is true that she's morally obliged to give one of A and C to Patient even though she neither believes of one of them that it is, nor presently has any evidence establishing that one of them is, the perfect cure, then it would be morally wrong to give anything other than one of A and C, even though her subjective circumstances don't indicate which of the drugs she's morally obliged to give to Patient.

Again, this line of argument can be resisted. Once again, it needn't be granted by the Subjectivist that Doctor would have that thought upon recognizing that she's forgotten which of A and C is the perfect cure, or they might maintain that though Doctor might have that thought, it would be mistaken. In this case, the Subjectivist might say, what Doctor might be doing is confusing the thought that she morally ought not to have forgotten which drug was the perfect cure (or rather she should have taken steps to ensure that she wouldn't have forgotten) for the thought that she did something morally wrong in giving drug B in the situation in which she found herself at the time of choice. If that's right, then the reflection upon her forgetting, were she to have it, would not be evidence of the falsity of Subjectivism.

A last attempt at this kind of argument against Subjectivism appeals to the purported veridicality of certain retrospective judgments of Doctor in certain versions of *Doctor*. Imagine that after administering B to Patient, Doctor discovers that A was the perfect cure. In such circumstances she might have the thought, "Ack! I now see that what I morally ought to have done was administer A. I just didn't know at the time that that was what I morally ought to have done." If this thought is not mistaken, then that, once again, would put pressure on the Subjectivist position.

As should be obvious by now, this line of argument too is not decisive. A Subjectivist can simply reply that Doctor needn't have any such thought or that though she might, that thought would be mistaken. A Subjectivist might plausibly suggest that Doctor wouldn't think that she had acted wrongly in giving drug B. Rather, she might instead have the following, equally natural thought: "Well, I know I did the right thing in giving Patient drug B, because that was the safest bet at the time. True, giving him A would have had a better result, but what I ought to have done in my circumstances is exactly what I did." And, surely, it would be natural for others to reassure Doctor by telling her, "Don't worry, you did the right thing," were she to doubt that she acted morally rightly in administering drug B as she did. So, retrospective judgments of the sort around which this version of the argument against Subjectivism are based don't seem strong enough to refute Subjectivism.

The argument against Subjectivism based on these various possible reflections by Doctor in various iterations of *Doctor* all depend on the strength of the intuitions both that Doctor might have the thoughts in question in each of the cases and that those thoughts would be veridical. But as we've seen, they can most certainly be contested.[31]

4.2 The Gathering-More-Evidence Argument against Subjectivism

Another argument against Subjectivism appeals to the thought that sometimes, it seems, being morally conscientious requires seeking out more evidence. But the Subjectivist, so goes the argument, has a hard time accounting for this. Take *Doctor* once more. Suppose Doctor has a manual in which she knows she can look and discover which of medicine A and medicine C is the complete cure and which the fatal poison. In this version of the case, you might think, the only morally conscientious thing for Doctor to do is check in the manual to see which is the complete cure. In such circumstances, it would be morally wrong for Doctor to GIVE B. But why, according to Subjectivists, would that be the case? By stipulation, in this version of the case, Doctor has the same evidence, prior to looking in the manual, about which of medicine A and medicine C is the complete cure and which the fatal poison as she does in the original version of the case, and so if that evidence supported the moral permissibility of her doing GIVE B in the original version of the case, that too, according to the Subjectivist, should support her doing GIVE B in this version of the case. But if that were right, then it should be perfectly consistent with moral

---

[31] Kiesewetter (2011) and Lord (2015) embrace replies of the sorts considered in this section to this first argument against Subjectivism.

conscientiousness for Doctor to GIVE B in this new version of the case. As it isn't, so goes the argument, that shows that Subjectivism is false.[32]

The Subjectivist has a ready reply to this argument. The proponent of this argument is overlooking the fact that in this new version of the case, Doctor has another option among those between which she is choosing at the time of action:

> CHECK: check in the manual to see which of medicine A and medicine C is the complete cure

And the Subjectivist could rightly suggest that their version of the correct moral theory can accommodate the thought that moral conscientiousness requires looking in the manual by appeal to their preferred version of Subjectivism. In particular, if a Subjectivist appealed to the thought that what a person is morally obligated to do is maximize expected deontic value, they could well say that in the new version of the case, GIVE B no longer maximizes expected deontic value; in the new version of the case, CHECK is the option that maximizes expected deontic value because their evidence indicates that were she to CHECK, she would then come to know which was the perfect cure and then go on to administer it – and that, we can suppose, has a much higher deontic value than does her merely partially curing Patient by doing GIVE B. But if that's the case, then it will follow from the Subjectivist's preferred version of Subjectivism that it would be wrong to GIVE B, and in fact wrong to do anything other than CHECK in the new version of the case – and that, they might say, explains why being morally conscientious requires doing CHECK. The argument against Subjectivism by appeal to the need to acquire more evidence, then, falls apart.

4.3 The Lucky Guess Argument against Subjectivism

A slightly different kind of argument against Subjectivism also takes as its starting point the situation in *Doctor*. Suppose, in a momentary lapse in moral conscientiousness, Doctor prescribes medicine A despite the fact that she does not know, or have any evidence, that A, rather than C, is the perfect cure. As A is in fact the perfect cure, after administering it, Patient will be completely cured. In recovering her moral conscientiousness after the fact, Doctor will no doubt chastise herself for having acted as riskily as she did. But, and here's the point, she won't wish she had acted any differently than she in fact did. If anything, she'll be grateful for the fact that she morally unconscientiously chose to GIVE A. She won't instead wish she had been morally conscientious and given Patient medicine B, for as a morally conscientious agent she is unconcerned with her

---

[32] Something like this argument is considered (and rejected) in Howard-Snyder (2005).

own moral conscientiousness; a concern with her own moral conscientious-ness – past, present, or future – would be a kind of moral self-indulgence with which the morally conscientious person has no truck. This fact can be leveraged into an argument against Subjectivism. If an agent is truly morally conscien-tious, then they are concerned never to act wrongly. And this concern not to act wrongly concerns their entire life – past, present, and future. They hope not to act wrongly not only in the present but in the future as well. And if they have acted wrongly in the past, they'll wish they hadn't done so. As Doctor would not wish she had acted any differently than she in fact did in the version of the case in which she unconscientiously administers A to Patient, that's a sign, then, that it was not morally wrong of her to GIVE A. But, as on any plausible Subjectivism about moral wrongness it would be morally wrong for Doctor not to GIVE B in *Doctor*, Subjectivism is false.

But mightn't part of her wish that she had acted differently than GIVE A? Plausibly not. Though she'll be angry with herself for having done so, she won't wish, in any sense, that she had acted any differently than she in fact did. To see this, consider another version of a Jackson-style case where the consequence of the uncontroversially morally conscientious option is one for which the stakes are higher than they are for administering B in *Doctor*:

> **Miners**: Ten miners are trapped either in shaft *A* or in shaft *B*, but we do not know which. Flood waters threaten to flood the shafts. We have enough sandbags to block one shaft, but not both. If we block one shaft, all the water will go into the other shaft, killing any miners inside it. If we block neither shaft, both shafts will fill halfway with water, and just one miner, the lowest in the shaft, will be killed. (Kolodny and MacFarlane 2010: 115)[33]

If, in a moment of unconscientiousness, we block one of the shafts, and luckily it turns out to be the shaft with the miners in it, we won't afterwards wish we had blocked neither of the shafts (even though that would obviously have been the morally conscientious thing for us to have done at the time), resulting in the death of one of the miners. Instead, we'll be glad we unconscientiously did that which saved all of the miners. Again, that we'll be glad we blocked the shaft we did and not wish we hadn't puts pressure on the thought that it was morally wrong of us, as any plausible Subjectivism would have it, to block the shaft we in fact did.[34]

---

[33] This case was originally presented in Parfit (2011). (That it is discussed in Kolodny and MacFarlane (2010) is explained by the fact that the manuscript for Parfit (2011) was in circula-tion many years before it was published in 2011.) The original presentation of this kind of case is credited by Parfit to Regan (1980).

[34] True, we might feel somewhat guilty for having blocked the shaft that we did. But, I'm claiming, the fact that we wouldn't wish we had acted any differently than we in fact did act suggests that

This argument might be resisted as follows. It might be maintained that though we and Doctor might not wish we had acted differently than we did, this doesn't spell trouble for Subjectivism. It might be maintained that the fact we wouldn't, after regaining our moral conscientiousness, wish we had acted differently doesn't indicate that in acting as we did, we didn't act morally wrongly. The reason why we wouldn't wish we had acted differently can be explained by appeal to something other than the fact that acting in any other way than we in fact acted would have been morally wrong. For instance, it might be argued, it is because our doing what we did had the best consequences that explains why we, once we regained our moral conscientiousness, wouldn't wish we had acted differently and why we would be glad we acted as we did.

The plausibility of this reply obviously depends heavily on the plausibility of the Subjectivist's alternative explanation of why, in recovering our moral conscientiousness, we wouldn't wish we had acted differently in *Miners*. To put pressure on it, we can consider other cases in which an appeal to the goodness of the consequences of what we morally unconscientiously do can't explain our not wishing we had acted differently.

> **Promise**: On Monday evening Promisor solemnly promises Promisee that she will go over to his house for dinner Tuesday evening. Promisor would prefer to have dinner with Friend instead of Promisee, however. Dinner with Friend will be far more enjoyable for all parties involved than would dinner with Promisee. In fact, though Promisor has neither promised Friend that she would come over for dinner nor given any indication to Friend that she will, Friend is expecting Promisor to come for dinner and will be just as disappointed if she doesn't show up as Promisee will be if she has dinner with Friend instead. On Tuesday evening, in a temporary lapse in moral conscientiousness, Promisor sets off to have dinner with Friend instead of Promisee. Because she has mistaken Promisee's address for Friend's address, however, she arrives at Promisee's house and thus ends up having dinner with him instead of with Friend.

In this case, when she regains her moral conscientiousness, Promisor will not wish she had acted differently than she in fact did. Being morally conscientious, she'll be glad she ended up doing that which she promised Promisee she would do even though when she acted she did what any plausible Subjectivism would declare morally wrong. In *Promise*, unlike in *Doctor* and in *Miners*, a Subjectivist can't appeal to the goodness of the consequences of acting as

---

Subjectivism is false. And that's because, plausibly, if one had acted wrongly, one will wish, once one regains one's moral conscientiousness, that one had acted differently, given that moral conscientiousness constitutively involves an aversion to acting wrongly, in the sense of "wrongly" with which the morally conscientious person is concerned in their deliberations about what to do.

she did to explain why she wouldn't wish she had acted differently because the consequences of her acting as she did are worse overall than they would have been had she acted differently. So what explains why she wouldn't wish she had acted any differently than she in fact had?

A Subjectivist could presumably maintain that what explains why Promisor would not wish she had acted differently than she in fact did in *Promise* once she regains her moral conscientiousness is that as a morally conscientious agent, she'll want to do what she promised Promisee she would do, and only by doing what she in fact did would she have done so. But it can't simply be that her desire to do what she promised Promisee to do explains why she wouldn't wish she had acted differently, for there are versions of the case in which she would indeed wish she had acted differently even though acting as she did did in fact result in her doing what she promised to do. For instance, consider a version of the case in which, on Tuesday morning, Promisee releases Promisor from her promise to have dinner with him that evening. In such a version of the case Promisor might indeed wish she had acted differently than she in fact did, and that's true even though only doing what she in fact did would have resulted in her doing what she promised to do.

Maybe what she, as she recovers her moral conscientiousness, would want is that she did whatever she made a promise, *from which she has not been released*, to do. But even that can't be what truly explains why in *Promise* she does not wish she acted differently than she actually did, for if it were the case that some other stronger objective *pro tanto* duty, one that opposed her doing what she promised Promisee to do, were in play, then she might well wish she had acted differently than she in fact did in *Promise*. What the Subjectivist is going to have to do to explain why it is that, after regaining her moral conscientiousness, she wouldn't wish she had acted differently in *Promise* is to appeal to her desire as a morally conscientious agent not to have acted in a way that satisfies any disjunct of the (potentially very) disjunctive supervenience base for the objective wrongness of her action. At this point, however, the Subjectivist's explanation may seem decidedly weaker than that of the Objectivist's, according to which what explains why Promisor doesn't wish she had acted differently than she in fact did in *Promise* is that in acting in any other way than the way she did in fact act would have been morally wrong. In general, a unified explanation of a phenomenon is more satisfying than a (potentially wildly) disjunctive one: an appeal to a desire not to act wrongly as the explanation of why Promisor does not wish she had acted any differently than she in fact did thus is better than an appeal to a desire not to act in one of many different, non-deontically described ways of acting that constitute the supervenience base of an action's being objectively morally wrong. If the former explanation of why, after regaining her moral conscientiousness, Promisor would not wish she had acted differently than she did is better, then that might indeed suggest that Subjectivism is false.

4.4 The Advice Argument against Subjectivism

Yet another argument against Subjectivism about moral wrongness is based on the phenomenon of advice. Suppose Doctor in her situation in *Doctor* can ask her colleague, Colleague, which medicine she ought to give her patient and suppose Colleague knows that medicine A is the complete cure and medicine C is the fatal poison. In such a situation it seems intuitively the correct answer for Colleague to give Doctor that she morally ought to GIVE A. But, you might think, the answer to her question "which medicine morally ought I to give Patient?" she is looking for when she asks it of Colleague is the same as the answer to that question she is looking for when she asks it of herself in the midst of her deliberations about what to do. But if that's right, then, as giving Patient medicine A is according to Subjectivism morally wrong, that suggests that Subjectivism about moral wrongness is false, for it seems, then, that the notion of wrongness she is ultimately concerned to avoid in her deliberations about what to do is not the Subjectivist's notion.[35]

There are a couple of replies to this argument. First, it has been denied that Colleague speaks truly when he responds to Doctor's question by saying she morally ought to GIVE A (Zimmerman 2006, 2008). The reason why it seems that Colleague does speak truly when he says she morally ought to GIVE A, according to this reply, is that saying that she ought to GIVE A is what is morally required of Colleague in the situation. Because Colleague himself is obliged to do the best he can for Patient, and the only way for him to achieve the best result for Patient is by getting Doctor to administer medicine A to Patient, it is morally required of Colleague to tell Doctor that she morally ought to GIVE A even though his saying so is strictly speaking false.

There are a couple of problems with this reply. First, the error theory offered for why it seems that Colleague answers Doctor's question correctly doesn't seem plausible. The error theory has it that in responding to Doctor's question Colleague is morally required to lie to Doctor. But the case doesn't seem to be one of morally obligatory lying. Second, and more importantly, the explanation of why Colleague seems to answer Doctor's question correctly is inadequate. In versions of the case in which Colleague, himself, does not have the moral obligation to do the best for Patient, and thus for which the error theory would predict it would not be correct for Colleague to tell Doctor that she

---

[35] This kind of argument appears in Thomson (1985, 1990, 2008) and Kolodny and MacFarlane (2010).

morally ought to GIVE A, it still seems as if the only correct answer for Colleague to give in response to Doctor's question is that she morally ought to GIVE A. Suppose, for instance, Colleague knows that if Doctor does not GIVE A, medicine A will be used to cure another patient of a similar condition. Plausibly in such a case Colleague does not have a moral obligation to prefer Patient to the other patient who would receive medicine A if Patient doesn't get it and so is not morally required to make sure that Patient, as opposed to the other patient, gets medicine A. Even in such a version of the case, however, it seems that Colleague only answers Doctor's question correctly by saying that what *she* morally ought to do is GIVE A. If Colleague knows that Doctor's obligation is to do the best she can for Patient, and not for the other patient, if Doctor does indeed ask, "which medicine morally ought I to give Patient?", then it seems Colleague can only answer correctly by saying "medicine A." But in such a case the purported error theory can't explain the correctness of that response, for in that case Colleague's answer is not something he is morally required to say on the basis of an obligation to do the best he can for Patient. That it is the only correct answer for Colleague to give can only be explained by the fact that it is true and Colleague is obliged to tell Doctor the truth in that situation.

Another reply (Kiesewetter 2017) to the argument from advice against Subjectivism is to explain the correctness of Colleague's answer not as an instance of morally obligatory lying but as a bit of self-fulfilling truth-telling. According to this reply, in answering that she morally ought to give Patient medicine A, Colleague anticipates that his answer to Doctor's question will give Doctor sufficient evidence to believe that medicine A is the complete cure and in virtue of her having that evidence on the basis of his answer to her question, according to Subjectivism, it will then be true that what Doctor morally ought to do in her situation is GIVE A.[36] According to this reply, then, Colleague's assertion that Doctor morally ought to GIVE A makes itself true according to Subjectivism because it, as it were, anticipates its own influence on Doctor's epistemic situation. Thus, so it is claimed, Subjectivism is consistent with the advice data and thus not refuted by it.

This reply also has problems. First, the explanation of the correctness of Colleague's answer is dubious. The reply only works on the assumption that, in

---

[36] Kiesewetter's (2017) version of this reply has it that not only will it be true *after* Colleague says that Doctor morally ought to GIVE A that she then morally ought to GIVE A, but also *as*, and even *before*, he says it, for the answer to the question being asked of Colleague – what she, at the time of asking, ought to later do, at the time of action – Kiesewetter maintains, is determined by what it *will* be the case that she ought to do at the time of action were she to do everything she ought to do between the time of the asking and the time of action. The problems I go on to suggest plague the reply considered in the text likewise plague Kiesewetter's version of the reply.

answering that she morally ought to GIVE A, Colleague's answer provides Doctor with sufficient evidence that medicine A is the complete cure so as to make it the thing she morally ought to do given the truth of Subjectivism. But consider a slight variant of that case. Suppose Colleague knows that Doctor has tons of misleading evidence that he is an inveterate liar. In such a case, Colleague would know that his saying that she morally ought to GIVE A won't tip Doctor's evidential scales in the direction of medicine A's being the complete cure. If the alternative explanation proposed by the reply under consideration were correct, in this version of the case it should seem intuitive that Colleague answers incorrectly, indeed falsely, when he says that Doctor ought to GIVE A. But it doesn't intuitively seem that Colleague answers incorrectly or falsely when he says that Doctor ought to GIVE A in such a version of the case.[37]

Second, this reply has unpalatable consequences in the case in which Doctor has overwhelming evidence both that Colleague is a reliable source and that he knows which of the medicines is the complete cure and which the poison. In such circumstances, the reply under consideration has it that it would not only be correct for Colleague to say that Doctor ought to GIVE C, the lethal poison, but also that were he to do so, he would be speaking truly. This is because, given that Colleague knows that Doctor's evidence has it that Colleague is a reliable source and one Doctor has strong evidence knows what the complete cure is, Colleague knows that whatever he says Doctor morally ought to do will come out true according to Subjectivism. In such a case, just uttering that Doctor morally ought to GIVE C is enough to tip the evidential scales for Doctor in such a way as to make it the case that giving medicine C to Patient is what she morally ought to do according to Subjectivism. That's hard to stomach. Could Colleague really truly and correctly say to Doctor that she morally ought to give Patient that which he knows is the fatal poison?

This reply, it can be argued then, fails twice over: it can't truly accommodate the intuition that Colleague speaks correctly when he says that what Doctor morally ought to do is GIVE A, and it also yields the result that Colleague would speak truly and correctly were he to say that Doctor morally ought to GIVE C. If this is right, then the argument from advice against Subjectivism can withstand this reply to it.

4.5 The Options Argument against Subjectivism

Another argument against Subjectivism is that it is incompatible with the conjunction of the following two facts: (a) that what it would be morally

---

[37] Kolodny and MacFarlane (2010) offer this kind of response.

wrong for one to do is (at least partly) grounded in the options one has at the time of one's choice, and (b) that what options one has at the time of one's choice is not fully grounded in one's subjective circumstances. What it would be morally wrong for one to do clearly depends on all of the options one has. For example, if one faces a choice between (1) doing nothing and (2) rescuing A at no cost to oneself, then (2) is not morally wrong (in fact, it is morally required). But if one faces a choice between (1) doing nothing, (2) rescuing A at no cost to oneself, and (3) rescuing A and B at no cost to oneself, then (2) is indeed morally wrong ((3) is clearly morally required in such a case). So, the moral wrongness of an agent's action is at least partly grounded in the options they have at the time of its performance. But, so goes the argument against Subjectivism, what a person's options are at the time of action is not fully grounded in their subjective circumstances.[38]

What one can do is something that can surely be outside of one's own ken. For instance, two people might be mentally exactly identical, but though one of them can raise their hand, the other, because of some unforeseen and undetected momentary paralysis, cannot. For another example, consider an assassin and their brain-in-a-vat twin. A brain-in-a-vat twin is a being who is identical in all subjective circumstances to the one with whom they are a twin, though they and their twin's objective circumstances are radically different: for instance, whereas the assassin has arms and legs, and routinely assassinates people, their brain-in-a-vat twin has no arms or legs, and never assassinates anyone; it just floats in the vat, being stimulated by the electrodes that ensure it is subjectively indistinguishable from the assassin. Now, the options facing the assassin and their brain-in-a-vat twin are different: whereas the assassin may face a choice between either stabbing their victim or not, though their brain-in-a-vat twin might think it is facing the very same choice, as it clearly has no knife, or even a hand with which to wield it, it does not actually have the option of stabbing its victim, or anyone for that matter. If all of this is right, then Subjectivism is false; what it would be morally wrong for one to do is grounded partly in the options one has and the options one has are at least partly grounded in one's objective circumstances.

Now, mightn't a Subjectivist reply to this argument in the following way? True, the assassin and their brain-and-a-vat twin have different options before them, but *as regards the options that have moral status*, they do not differ. A Subjectivist might maintain that the only things we ever do that are morally right or morally wrong are the basic mental actions we perform – those mental

---

[38] Zimmerman (2008) raises this kind of worry for Subjectivism. Graham (2010) makes this argument.

actions by which we perform all the actions we perform and which themselves are not performed by us by performing yet other actions. A common example of a basic mental action is *choosing* to do something. Another common candidate for a basic mental action is *trying* to do a certain thing. Whether one goes in for choosings or tryings as one's central basic mental action, surely there must be some such actions; if there weren't basic actions – things we do directly, not by doing anything else – then it would take infinitely many actions to perform any action, and that's implausible. It is also plausible that the basic actions we perform, whatever they are, are mental, for that surely is where agency begins. We can perform the mental action of choosing (trying) to stand up and often, if not always, when we do stand up it is *by* choosing (trying) to stand up that we come to stand up; our standing up is caused (in the right way) by our choosing (trying) to stand up.[39] Picking up on this distinction between basic and nonbasic actions, and accepting that it is only mental basic actions that have any moral status, a Subjectivist might claim that, contra the argument against Subjectivism by way of the (at least partial) objectivity of an agent's options, the options between which an agent in the first instance ever decides are indeed grounded fully in their subjective circumstances. And this, they might maintain, is because either it is necessarily true that for any ϕ, any agent that can conceive of ϕing is able to choose (try) to ϕ, or it is necessarily true that whether one is able to choose (try) to ϕ is always apparent to one from one's own subjective circumstances.

According to this reply, though the assassin is able to assassinate their victim, and we might suppose actually does so, and their brain-in-a-vat twin neither does, nor is able to, assassinate anyone, they both do face a choice between the same options as regards the basic actions they are deciding between; viz., doing nothing and choosing to assassinate someone. And it is only one's choosings and one's failures to choose that are, in the first instance, morally wrong. The brain-in-a-vat twin of the assassin just as much chooses to assassinate someone as the assassin does, and that choice is just as morally wrong as is the choice of the assassin. Again, true, the assassin does end up assassinating someone and the brain-in-a-vat twin does not, and so while there are some things that the assassin does and is able to do that the brain-in-a-vat twin does not and cannot do, the moral status of the actions of theirs that have moral status, either *tout court* or in the first instance, is the same.

Hedden (2012) is one who argues for a version of the view that the only actions we perform that have any moral status are basic actions, and he considers

---

[39] The picture of action with which I am working here is one that lies within the causal theory of action, which has as its modern locus classicus Davidson (1963).

decisions to be the basic actions that are such as to have any moral status at all. He argues that the correct account of the options one faces when performing a deontically evaluable action must satisfy three desiderata: that the agent's options include only actions they are able to perform (the "ought" implies "can" desideratum), that the agent be such as to believe of every option that they have that they can perform it (the transparency desideratum), and that whether they can perform the action in question supervenes on the desires and beliefs of the agent (the supervenience desideratum). Only the view that Hedden calls Options-as-Decisions – the view that the only deontically evaluable options one ever has are constituted by the particular decisions one is able to make – satisfies all three desiderata. Koon (2019), however, shows both that Options-as-Decisions falls prey to Frankfurtian counterexamples and that the transparency and supervenience desiderata are not jointly satisfiable. Koon's conclusion is the title of his paper, "Options Must Be External"; or, in other words, what options one has are not fully grounded in one's subjective circumstances.

Koon thus shows why Hedden's Options-as-Decisions won't work. And Options-as-Decisions, or any such similar view in terms of choosings or tryings, is implausible on its face. For, while it is plausible that some such things as choosings or tryings (or decidings) are the basic actions by which we perform any and all of the other actions we perform, it isn't plausible that the only actions we perform that have moral status are those basic actions. We're morally required not to murder, not merely not to choose, or try, to murder.[40] And it's simply not plausible either that it is necessarily true that for any ϕ, any agent that can conceive of ϕing is able to choose (try) to ϕ, or that it is necessarily true that whether one is able to choose (try) to ϕ is always apparent to one from one's subjective circumstances. Just as one can be unable to do something – raise one's hand, say – so too it is plausible that under certain circumstances one might be unable to even choose (try) to raise one's hand. Just as there might be paralysis at the level of bodily movements, so, too, it seems plausible that there could be paralysis at the level of choosings (or tryings). An example here might be a very severe arachnophobe – not only can they not bring themself to touch a spider, they can't even bring themself to choose to touch one.[41] And, what's

---

[40] It may well be that to murder someone, one must choose to murder them. That is, it may be that choosing to murder someone is a necessary part of murdering them. But, clearly, choosing to murder someone is not to murder them, for one can choose to murder someone while failing to actually murder them. My only claim here is that it is plausible that the moral requirement we're under is not merely the requirement not to choose to murder other people, but simply not to murder them. (There may indeed be a moral requirement not to choose to murder people, but as choosing to murder someone and murdering them are distinct, a requirement not to murder someone is distinct from a requirement not to choose to murder someone.)

[41] This case is of a kind made famous by Lehrer (1968) in offering a counterexample to the conditional analysis of ability.

more, not only might there be paralysis at the level of choosings (tryings), but such a paralysis needn't be evident to the one so paralyzed. Just as a person's legs might be paralyzed without them knowing it (think of the car accident victim just coming to after having been made paraplegic and knocked unconscious by the accident), so too might one's paralysis with respect to choosing be something about which one's evidence and beliefs are silent. But if one might indeed be unable to choose (try) to ϕ without having any evidence that one is unable to choose (try) to ϕ, then, contra this reply, one's options, even if they are restricted to one's choosings (or tryings), do indeed seem to be grounded, at least partly, in one's objective circumstances.

Insofar as Subjectivism is incompatible with the grounding of an agent's options, at least partly, in their objective circumstances, and as the wrongness of an agent's action is grounded, at least partly, in what options they have available to them, strict Subjectivism is false.

4.6 The Future Wrongdoing Argument against Subjectivism

Subjectivism has it that it would be morally wrong for Chen not to flip the switch in *Switch*. Another argument against Subjectivism counsels a closer look both at *Switch* and the morally conscientious person's desire not to act wrongly across time. In particular, so goes this argument, not only is the morally conscientious person concerned not to act wrongly in the present, they are also concerned not to act wrongly in the future. In fact, the morally conscientious person's concern not to act wrongly in the present just is the very same concern they have to not act wrongly in the future. And we can show, so goes this argument, that the morally conscientious person's concern not to act wrongly at other times than the present – in particular, their concern not to act wrongly in the future – is a concern not to act morally wrongly in the Objectivist's sense. But if the kind of wrongness the morally conscientious person is concerned to avoid in the future just is the very same wrongness they are concerned to avoid in the present, and the kind of wrongness they are concerned to avoid in the future is objective moral wrongness, then the kind of moral wrongness they are concerned to avoid in the present is objective moral wrongness, and thus Subjectivism is false.[42] (By "objective wrongness" I just mean the kind of wrongness Objectivists think is that which it is the main concern of the morally conscientious person to avoid doing – the kind of wrongness that is grounded in the actual facts of an agent's situation.)

To see that the kind of wrongness that a morally conscientious person is ultimately concerned to avoid is objective moral wrongness, consider:

---

[42] Graham (forthcoming) offers a version of this kind of argument.

Before Switch: At t_1, an hour prior to the obtaining of the state of affairs described in *Switch*, Chen knows that in one hour, at t_2, she will find herself in the situation described in *Switch*. She knows at t_1 both that at t_2 the light switch will be hooked up to a bomb and that at t_2 she will believe in accord with her evidence at t_2 that the light switch is not hooked up to a bomb – at t_1, Chen knows that in between t_1 and t_2 she will forget that the light switch is connected to the bomb (because, as she knows at t_1, some dastardly third party will inject her with a temporary amnesia-inducing drug between t_1 and t_2). At t_1, Chen faces a choice whether to pinch Tran or not. Chen knows at t_1 that if she pinches Tran at t_1, then at t_2 she will voluntarily refrain from flipping the switch then. Chen also knows that if she refrains from pinching Tran at t_1, then at t_2 she will voluntarily flip the switch out of a desire to help Gomez find her wallet.

If she is morally conscientious at t_1, Chen will pinch Tran at t_1. She will do this because she wants to make sure that she doesn't flip the switch at t_2, and she knows that the only thing that she can at t_1 do at t_1 that will lead to her not flipping the switch at t_2 is her pinching Tran at t_1. Now, note, pinching Tran at t_1 is morally wrong, both objectively and subjectively. Why? It is objectively wrong because there is a course of action available to her at t_1 in which she does not pinch Tran at t_1 or hurt anyone at t_2 – there is nothing preventing her from performing the course of action of refraining from pinching Tran at t_1 and then not flipping the switch at t_2, after all. It is also subjectively wrong for Chen to pinch Tran at t_1 because, according to both her beliefs and all of her evidence at t_1, she has a course of action available to her in which she neither pinches Tran nor hurts anyone at t_2 – she believes, and her evidence indicates, at t_1 that she is able at t_1 to perform the course of action of not pinching Tran at t_1 and not flipping the switch at t_2. So Chen's pinching Tran at t_1 is clearly morally wrong in the sense of "wrong" that is of concern to the morally conscientious person.[43] If Chen's pinching Tran at t_1 is both objectively and subjectively morally wrong, then how is it that if she is morally conscientious at t_1, Chen will pinch Tran then? She will do so because, though it is morally wrong for her to pinch Tran at t_1, given that she, as a morally conscientious agent, is concerned not to act wrongly, both in the present and in the future, she will accept her doing of something minorly morally wrong in the present in exchange for her avoiding doing something much more seriously morally wrong in the future.[44]

---

[43] I'm here assuming the truth of Possibilism in the argument against Subjectivism about moral wrongness. One could thus contest this argument by rejecting Possibilism in favor of Actualism. This will not work, however. Actualism is false. See Zimmerman (1996) and Graham (2019) for arguments against Actualism.

[44] *Before Switch* is thus another counterexample to ***No Deliberate Conscientious Wrongdoing***, one of the two conceptions of moral conscientiousness discussed at length in Section 3.

But notice, Chen's flipping the switch at t_2 in *Before Switch* is only morally wrong according to the Objectivist's notion of wrongness. Recall that for the Subjectivist, Chen acts perfectly morally permissibly, even obligatorily, in flipping the switch in *Switch*, and, thus, it is morally permissible for her to flip the switch at t_2 after not pinching Tran at t_1 in *Before Switch*. So, it seems, as a morally conscientious agent, she is certainly concerned not to do what is morally wrong in the Objectivist's sense, at least in the future. Not only is she concerned very much not to act wrongly in the future in the Objectivist's sense, she is not at all concerned to not act wrongly in the Subjectivist's sense. To see that she is utterly unconcerned with not acting morally wrongly in the future, in the Subjectivist's sense, consider:

> **Sore Throat:** Mbeki is suffering from a mildly painful sore throat. Lopez is carrying a revolver that at t_1 she knows shall forever remain unloaded. At t_1 she knows that if she points the revolver at Mbeki and pulls the trigger at t_2, her doing so will both cause Mbeki no harm and cure his sore throat. (How will pointing the revolver at Mbeki and pulling the trigger cause his sore throat to be cured? Suppose that pulling the trigger while pointing the revolver at him will somehow remotely release some medicine into his throat.) Lopez also knows at t_1 that between t_1 and t_2 she will come to believe, in accord with her evidence, but contrary to the actual facts, then, that the revolver is loaded. Lopez knows at t_1 that if she swallows a rage-inducing pill at t_1, at t_2 she will voluntarily point the revolver at Mbeki and pull the trigger.[45] Finally, Lopez also knows that if she does not swallow the pill at t_1, at t_2 she will neither point the revolver at Mbeki nor pull the trigger. (Suppose that Lopez knows at t_1 that, were she to swallow the pill at t_1 and then go on to point the revolver at Mbeki and pull the trigger at t_2, she would do so unobserved by anyone else, including Mbeki, and also that, were she to do so, after doing so she would immediately regain her moral conscientiousness and forget that she ever pointed what she thought was a loaded revolver at an innocent person and pulled the trigger.)

In this case Lopez, if she is morally conscientious, will swallow the pill at t_1. But here, as a morally conscientious agent, she is totally unconcerned with acting morally wrongly in the Subjectivist's sense in the future, and very much concerned to not act morally wrongly in the Objectivist's sense in the future. She can only be morally conscientious by doing that which she knows will lead to her acting very seriously morally wrongly at t_2 in the Subjectivist's sense. But if the morally conscientious person's concern not to act wrongly in their

---

[45] In saying that she knows at t_1 that if she swallows the pill at t_1, at t_2 she will *voluntarily* point the revolver at Mbeki and pull the trigger, I mean that she knows that if she swallows the pill at t_1, she will at t_2 point the revolver at Mbeki and pull the trigger while at the same time, at t_2, being able to refrain from pointing the revolver at Mbeki and pulling the trigger.

deliberations about what to do in the present just is the very same concern they have not to act wrongly in the future, then the fact that they are utterly unconcerned with acting subjectively morally wrongly in the future is an indication that the wrongness they are ultimately concerned to avoid doing in their deliberations about what to do in the present is not the Subjectivist's notion of wrongness. So, if the concern about the future just is the concern about the present, and Lopez is very concerned not to act wrongly in the future in the Objectivist's sense – she is willing to swallow the pill at t_1, thereby causing herself to voluntarily do at t_2 what she then will think is killing an innocent person merely to avoid doing what is wrong in the Objectivist's sense, namely failing to alleviate Mbeki's mild suffering – it is very plausible that it is on the Objectivist's conception of wrongness, and not the Subjectivist's, that she is concerned not to act wrongly in her deliberations about what to do in the present.[46]

Mightn't one respond to this argument in the following way? "Sure, Chen would pinch Tran at t_1 in *Before Switch* and Lopez would swallow the rage-inducing pill at t_1 in *Sore Throat*, but that's because, as morally conscientious agents, they're concerned to minimize harm in the future, and only by doing those things will they minimize harm overall going forward." This reply offers an alternative explanation – other than the explanation in terms of which moral conscientiousness involves a concern to avoid acting wrongly in the Objectivist's sense in the future – of why being morally conscientious in both cases requires acting in those ways. If it's because they are, as morally conscientious agents, concerned to minimize harm overall that explains why they act as they do, then we can't infer that it is a concern to avoid acting wrongly in the Objectivist's sense that explains what moral conscientiousness requires in each of those cases.

---

[46] Here's another way of arguing against Subjectivism that's in the same spirit. The morally conscientious person's concern in their deliberations about what to do not to act morally wrongly is the same as their concern not to act wrongly throughout their entire life. However, in reflecting on the life they would rather lead between one in which they never act morally wrongly in the Subjectivist's sense but do frequently act wrongly, and sometimes very wrongly, in the Objectivist's sense and one in which they never act morally wrongly in the Objectivist's sense but do frequently act wrongly, and sometimes very wrongly, in the Subjectivist's sense, they would decidedly prefer the latter. And if given a choice between those two lives, without any specifics other than the deontic statuses of their actions just described, they'd most certainly choose the latter. But if that's right and the notion of wrongness with which they are concerned when they are concerned not to act wrongly throughout the course of their life is the Objectivist's notion, and the concern they have not to act wrongly throughout their life just is the same concern they have not to act wrongly in their deliberations about what to do in the present, then not acting wrongly according to the Objectivist's notion of wrongness, and not the Subjectivist's notion, is what is of ultimate concern to the morally conscientious person in their deliberations about what to do.

An appeal to a concern to minimize harm won't do, though, for it isn't the case that Chen and Lopez are motivated simply to minimize harm going forward. For were the twenty people the bomb would kill in *Before Switch* not innocent – and were themselves about to villainously kill four innocent children if they aren't prevented from doing so by being blown up by the bomb, say – it is not the case that to be morally conscientious Chen would have to pinch Tran at t_1. And this is true even though pinching Tran in such a version of the case would be the option at t_1 that would lead to the minimization of harm going forward (flipping the switch at t_2 after not pinching Tran at t_1 would lead to the death of twenty people, whereas not flipping the switch at t_2 after pinching Tran at t_1 would lead to the death of four people and Tran's having a sore arm).[47] And if Lopez had promised Mbeki at t_1 that she wouldn't heal his sore throat at t_2 – a promise she knows at t_1 she will have forgotten by t_2 – it would not be consistent with her being morally conscientious for her to swallow the rage-inducing pill at t_1 even though doing that would lead to the least harm overall – swallowing the pill at t_1 would lead to no suffering in the future, whereas not swallowing the pill at t_1 would lead to the continued mild suffering of Mbeki in the future.

So, one can't appeal to something like a desire to minimize harm overall to explain why it is that Chen and Lopez being morally conscientious requires their acting in the described ways. One could offer other rival explanations, of course, but, I submit, taking this tack would in the end require insisting that what motivates them to act as they do as morally conscientious agents, rather than being a desire to avoid acting wrongly in the Objectivist's sense in the future, is a desire to avoid acting in those ways that exemplify the non-deontic supervenience base of the Objectivist's conception of moral wrongness.[48] But the non-deontic supervenience base of the Objectivist's conception of moral wrongness will, given the plurality of factors deemed morally relevant by commonsense morality – harm minimization, benefit maximization, promising, truth-telling, consent, etc. – be rather widely disjunctive. And, I once again submit, an appeal to a desire to avoid acting objectively morally wrongly, rather than an appeal to a desire to avoid acting in those ways that exemplify the non-deontic supervenience base of objective moral wrongness, to explain why it is that moral conscientiousness requires Chen's pinching Tran at t_1 in *Before*

---

[47] One might think that allowing the killing of innocent children, though less harmful on a straightforward account of harmfulness than the killing of the twenty, is nonetheless a worse outcome than the killing of the twenty. Fair enough. But the challenge for this response to the argument is to come up with an account of this worseness of one state of affairs over another that isn't itself just a covert appeal to the wrongness of the action that brings it about.

[48] The dialectic here likely would mirror that highlighted in the discussion of the *Promise* case above.

Switch and Lopez's swallowing the pill at t_1 in *Sore Throat* is both more intuitively plausible and, on theoretical simplicity grounds, decidedly preferable.

Putting everything together, what we have, then, is an argument that the kind of wrongness that the morally conscientious person is concerned in their deliberations about what to do to avoid doing is that kind of wrongness that is grounded, as the Objectivist maintains, in the actual facts of the agent's situation – things like actual harm-causing, actual promise-keeping, actual consent-abiding, etc. – rather than the kind of wrongness that is grounded, as the Subjectivist maintains, in the facts concerning either the beliefs of, or the evidence possessed by, the agent in question – things like apparent harm-causing, evidence of promise-keeping, belief that one has another's consent, etc. But if that's right, then that's good grounds for thinking that Subjectivism is false.

These are some of the main arguments against Subjectivism about moral wrongness. As we've seen, while a number of them are, at best, inconclusive, others do seem to refute strict Subjectivism about moral wrongness. Ross's Argument depends on intuitions concerning the effect the acquisition of better information has on the wrongness of our actions that are clearly disputable. The Gathering-More-Evidence Argument rests on a failure to recognize that the gathering of more evidence is itself an action about which Subjectivism needn't be silent. The Lucky Guess Argument puts pressure on Subjectivism by way of a recognition that in *Doctor*-type cases in which the agent unconscientiously though luckily chooses that which they objectively morally ought to do, they won't, in any sense, wish that they acted differently than they did. The Advice Argument also puts significant pressure on Subjectivism by way of showing that Subjectivism has a difficult time accommodating data concerning advice in *Doctor*-type cases. The Options Argument arguably establishes the falsity of Subjectivism by showing that an accurate accounting of an agent's options entails that Subjectivism is false. And the Future Wrongdoing Argument arguably shows Subjectivism to be false by way of an examination of the morally conscientious person's concern not to act wrongly across time.

5 Objectivism or Ecumenism?

If Subjectivism is false, then either Objectivism or Ecumenism must be true. But which one? That depends on whether any of the arguments against Objectivism succeed. Now, I noted in my discussion of those arguments that though many of the arguments against Objectivism fail or are inconclusive, two of them, the last two, depend for their success on particular issues in the metaphysics of grounding. These arguments against Objectivism purport to show that Objectivism is incompatible with certain first-order moral judgments – the judgments that we can conditionalize our promises and our consent on features of our own mental lives and that certain kinds of moral risks are not morally obligatory. Only if the chains of grounding in question involved in each of the debates about these objections involve the same notion of grounding and that notion is transitive will these arguments against Objectivism go through. If they don't, either because the relevant notions of grounding are different or because the relevant notion of grounding is not transitive, then Objectivism, arguably, remains unscathed. On the other hand, if they do go through, then Ecumenism of some sort must be true.

Even if, because these anti-Objectivism arguments go through, Ecumenism, rather than Objectivism, is true, many questions of course still remain. But even so, I think it would nonetheless be true that though Ecumenism is the correct account of morality, the type of Ecumenism that would be true would be a predominantly objective Ecumenism. But what do I mean by "predominantly objective"? How does one measure the degree to which a moral theory is subjective or objective? I have no metric to use by which to measure the subjectiveness or objectiveness of a moral theory. Instead, I'll have to content myself with a rather rough and intuitive conception of the degree to which a theory is subjective or objective. Roughly, I think, the degree of subjectiveness of a moral theory depends on how often a fact in one's subjective circumstances is determinative of the moral status of one's act. And so, likewise, for the degree of objectiveness of a moral theory. I think, upon reflection, it is quite plausible that if Ecumenism is true, then it must be a predominantly objective Ecumenism.

Why? Well, the arguments against Objectivism that it was claimed have the best chance of working are arguments that depended on those very particular first-order normative judgments mentioned earlier. If it is true that because one can condition one's promise or consent to another on one's beliefs or on one's evidence's being a certain way, one can thereby make it the case that, in such instances, the moral status of one's actions is grounded in one's subjective circumstances, that only establishes that in those very particular circumstances does the moral status of one's action depend on one's subjective circumstances. And if it is true that because what one can do in the morally relevant sense depends on one's subjective circumstances, at least when it comes to one's own avoidance of harm in risky rescue situations, that only establishes that only when those conditions are in play will the moral status of one's action depend on one's subjective circumstances. So, though these anti-Objectivism arguments may indeed establish the falsity of strict Objectivism, if they do, they won't show that the true moral theory is all that subjective. The kinds of cases upon which these arguments against Objectivism are based are very particular and they do not establish that the moral status of our actions is all that frequently grounded in our subjective circumstances – conditional promising, conditional consent, and risky rescue cases constitute only one small portion of morality as a whole, after all.

I conclude that the true moral theory, whatever it happens to be, is either an objective one or an instance of a predominantly objective Ecumenism.

References

Berker, S. 2018. "The Unity of Grounding," *Mind*, 127: 729–77.

Bykvist, K. 2009. "Objective versus Subjective Moral Oughts," *Uppsala Philosophical Studies*, 57: 39–65.

Cohen, Y. and Timmerman, T. 2016. "Moral Obligations: Actualist, Possibilist, or Hybridist?" *Australasian Journal of Philosophy*, 94(4): 672–86.

Davidson, D. 1963. "Actions, Reasons, and Causes," *The Journal of Philosophy*, 60(23): 685–700.

Driver, J. 2012. "What the Objective Standard Is Good For," *Oxford Studies in Normative Ethics*, 2: 28–44.

Feldman, F. 1986. *Doing the Best We Can*. Dordrecht: D. Reidel.

Feldman, F. 2012. "True and Useful: On the Structure of a Two-Level Normative Theory," *Utilitas*, 24(2): 151–71.

Fine, K. 2012. "Guide to Ground," in F. Correia and B. Schnieder (eds.), *Metaphysical Grounding*. Cambridge: Cambridge University Press, 37–80.

Fox, P. 2019. "Revisiting the Argument from Action Guidance," *Journal of Ethics and Social Philosophy*, 15(3): 222–54.

Frankfurt, H. 1969. "Alternate Possibilities and Moral Responsibility," *The Journal of Philosophy*, 66(23): 829–39.

Goble, L. 1993. "The Logic of Obligation, 'Better' and 'Worse'," *Philosophical Studies*, 70: 133–63.

Goldman, H. S. 1976. "Dated Rightness and Moral Imperfection," *Philosophical Review*, 85: 449–87.

Goldman, H. S. 1978. "Doing the Best One Can," in A. I. Goldman and J. Kim (eds.), *Values and Morals*. Dordrecht: D. Reidel, 185–214.

Gowans, C. W. (ed.). 1987. *Moral Dilemmas*. New York: Oxford University Press.

Graham, P. A. 2010. "In Defense of Objectivism about Moral Obligation," *Ethics*, 121(1): 88–115.

Graham, P. A. 2014. "A Sketch of a Theory of Moral Blameworthiness," *Philosophy and Phenomenological Research*, 88(2): 388–409.

Graham, P. A. 2019. "An Argument for Objective Possibilism," *Ergo*, 6(8): 217–47.

Graham, P. A. in press. "Two Arguments for Objectivism about Moral Permissibility," *Australasian Journal of Philosophy*.

Greenspan, P. S. 1978. "Oughts and Determinism: A Response to Goldman," *Philosophical Review*, 87: 77–83.

Hedden, B. 2012. "Options and the Subjective *Ought*," *Philosophical Studies*, 158(2): 343–60.

Howard-Snyder, F. 2005. "It's the Thought That Counts," *Utilitas*, 17(3): 265–81.

Hurka, T. 2019. "More Seriously Wrong, More Importantly Right," *Journal of the American Philosophical Association*, 5(1): 41–58.

Jackson, F. 1991. "Decision-Theoretic Consequentialism and the Nearest and Dearest Objection," *Ethics*, 101(3): 461–82.

Jackson, F. and Pargetter, R. 1986. "Oughts, Options, and Actualism," *Philosophical Review*, 95: 233–55.

Kiesewetter, B. 2011. "'Ought' and the Perspective of the Agent," *Journal of Ethics and Social Philosophy*, 5(3): 1–24.

Kiesewetter, B. 2017. *The Normativity of Rationality*. Oxford: Oxford University Press.

Kolodny, N. and MacFarlane, J. 2010. "Ifs and Oughts," *The Journal of Philosophy*, 107(3): 115–43.

Koon, J. 2019. "Options Must Be External," *Philosophical Studies*, 177(5): 1175–89.

Lehrer, K. 1968. "Cans without Ifs," *Analysis*, 29: 29–32.

Litland, J. E. 2013. "On Some Counterexamples to the Transitivity of Grounding," *Essays in Philosophy*, 14(1): 19–32.

Lockhart, T. 2000. *Moral Uncertainty and Its Consequences*. Oxford: Oxford University Press.

Lord, E. 2015. "Acting for the Right Reasons, Abilities, and Obligation," *Oxford Studies in Metaethics*, 10: 26–52.

Lord, E. 2017. "What You're Rationally Required to Do and What You Ought to Do (Are the Same Thing!)," *Mind*, 126: 1109–54.

Lord, E. 2018. *The Importance of Being Rational*. Oxford: Oxford University Press.

Mason, E. 2013. "Objectivism and Prospectivism about Rightness," *Journal of Ethics and Social Philosophy*, 7(2): 1–21.

Mason, H. E. (ed.) 1996. *Moral Dilemmas and Moral Theory*. New York: Oxford University Press.

Moore, G. E. 1912. *Ethics*. Oxford: Oxford University Press.

Parfit, D. 2011. *On What Matters: Volume One*. Oxford: Oxford University Press.

Portmore, D. W. 2011. *Commonsense Consequentialism: Wherein Morality Meets Rationality*. New York: Oxford University Press.

Prichard, H. A. 2002. "Duty and Ignorance of Fact," in J. MacAdam (ed.), *Moral Writings*. Oxford: Oxford University Press, 84–101.

Prior, A. N. 1960. "The Autonomy of Ethics," *Australasian Journal of Philosophy*, 38(3). 199–206.

Regan, D. 1980. *Utilitarianism and Cooperation*. Oxford: Oxford University Press.

Rosen, G. 2010. "Metaphysical Dependence: Grounding and Reduction," in B. Hale and A. Hoffman (eds.), *Modality: Metaphysics, Logic, and Epistemology*. Oxford: Oxford University Press, 109–35.

Rosen, G. 2015. "The Alethic Conception of Moral Responsibility," in R. Clarke, M. McKenna, and A. Smith (eds.), *The Nature of Moral Responsibility: New Essays*. Oxford: Oxford University Press, 65–88.

Ross, J. 2012. "Actualism, Possibilism, and Beyond," *Oxford Studies in Normative Ethics*, 2: 74–96.

Ross, W. D. 1939. *Foundations of Ethics*. Oxford: Oxford University Press.

Ross, W. D. 2002. *The Right and the Good*. Oxford: Oxford University Press.

Scanlon, T. M. 2008. *Moral Dimensions: Permissibility, Meaning, and Blame*. Cambridge, MA: Harvard University Press.

Schaffer, J. 2012. "Grounding, Transitivity, and Contrastivity," in F. Correia and B Schnieder (eds.), *Metaphysical Grounding*. Cambridge: Cambridge University Press, 122–38.

Sepielli, A. 2012. "Subjective Normativity and Action Guidance," *Oxford Studies in Normative Ethics*, 2: 45–73.

Sepielli, A. 2018. "Subjective and Objective Reasons," in D. Star (ed.), *The Oxford Handbook of Reasons and Normativity*. Oxford: Oxford University Press, 784–99.

Sinnott-Armstrong, W. 1988. *Moral Dilemmas*. Oxford: Blackwell.

Smith, H. 2018. *Making Morality Work*. Oxford: Oxford University Press.

Sobel, J. H. 1976. "Utilitarianism and Past and Future Mistakes," *Noûs*, 10: 195–219.

Strawson, P. F. 1962. "Freedom and Resentment," *Proceedings of the British Academy*, 48: 1–25.

Thomason, R. H. 1981. "Deontic Logic and the Role of Freedom in Moral Deliberation," in R. Hilpinen (ed.), *New Studies in Deontic Logic*. Dordrecht: D. Reidel, 177–86.

Thomson, J. J. 1985. "Imposing Risks," in M. Gibson (ed.), *To Breathe Freely*. Totowa, NJ: Rowman and Allanheld, 124–40.

Thomson, J. J. 1990. *The Realm of Rights*. Cambridge, MA: Harvard University Press.

Thomson, J. J. 2008. *Normativity*. Peru, IL: Carus Publishing Company.

Vessel, J. P. 2009. "Defending a Possibilist Insight in Consequentialist Thought," *Philosophical Studies*, 142: 183–95.

Vorobej, M. 2000. "Prosaic Possibilism," *Philosophical Studies*, 97: 131–6.

Wallace, R. J. 1994. *Responsibility and the Moral Sentiments*. Cambridge, MA: Harvard University Press.

Way, J. and Whiting, D. 2016. "If You Justifiably Believe You Ought to ϕ, Then You Ought to ϕ," *Philosophical Studies*, 173(7): 1873–95.

Way, J. and Whiting, D. 2017. "Perspectivism and the Argument from Guidance," *Ethical Theory and Moral Practice*, 20(2): 361–74.

Zimmerman, M. J. 1988. *An Essay on Moral Responsibility*. Totowa, NJ: Rowman & Littlefield.

Zimmerman, M. J. 1996. *The Concept of Moral Obligation*. Cambridge: Cambridge University Press.

Zimmerman, M. J. 2006. "Is Moral Obligation Objective or Subjective?" *Utilitas*, 18(4): 329–61.

Zimmerman, M. J. 2008. *Living with Uncertainty*. Cambridge: Cambridge University Press.

Zimmerman, M. J. 2014. *Ignorance and Moral Obligation*. Oxford: Oxford University Press.

Cambridge Elements

Ethics

Ben Eggleston
University of Kansas

Ben Eggleston is a professor of philosophy at the University of Kansas. He is the editor of *John Stuart Mill, Utilitarianism: With Related Remarks from Mill's Other Writings* (Hackett, 2017) and a co-editor of *Moral Theory and Climate Change: Ethical Perspectives on a Warming Planet* (Routledge, 2020), *The Cambridge Companion to Utilitarianism* (Cambridge, 2014), and *John Stuart Mill and the Art of Life* (Oxford, 2011). He is also the author of numerous articles and book chapters on various topics in ethics.

Dale E. Miller
Old Dominion University, Virginia

Dale E. Miller is a professor of philosophy at Old Dominion University. He is the author of *John Stuart Mill: Moral, Social and Political Thought* (Polity, 2010) and a co-editor of *Moral Theory and Climate Change: Ethical Perspectives on a Warming Planet* (Routledge, 2020), *A Companion to Mill* (Blackwell, 2017), *The Cambridge Companion to Utilitarianism* (Cambridge, 2014), *John Stuart Mill and the Art of Life* (Oxford, 2011), and *Morality, Rules, and Consequences: A Critical Reader* (Edinburgh, 2000). He is also the editor-in-chief of *Utilitas*, and the author of numerous articles and book chapters on various topics in ethics broadly construed.

About the Series
This Elements series provides an extensive overview of major figures, theories, and concepts in the field of ethics. Each entry in the series acquaints students with the main aspects of its topic while articulating the author's distinctive viewpoint in a manner that will interest researchers.

Cambridge Elements ☰

Ethics

Elements in the Series

A full series listing is available at www.cambridge.org/EETH

Printed in the United States
by Baker & Taylor Publisher Services